Edinburgh

an intimate city

an illustrated anthology of
contemporary poetry about Edinburgh

Editors: Bashabi Fraser & Elaine Greig
Designed by Kirsty Wilson, Heritage and Arts Design Section

British Library Cataloguing in Publication Data
A catalogue record of this book is available from the British Library

Typeset in Humanist 521 BT and Adobe Garamond
Printed and bound by Print Services Unit, Murrayburn

ISBN No: 0 905072 93 6

The City of Edinburgh Council acknowledges subsidy from the
Scottish Arts Council towards the publication of this volume

Front cover illustrations:
Edinburgh by Sara Ogilvie
Grassmarket (detail) by Michael McVeigh

Back cover illustration:
The Enchanted Capital of Scotland by Jessie Marion King (1875 - 1949)

Contents

St. Andrew Square - the Banks by Ernest Lumsden (1883 - 1948)

Preface

Language is the proper medium of all our ideas and sentiments

Thomas Blacklock (1721-1791)

Edinburgh has been a source of fascination and inspiration to writers for centuries. Few other cities have quite so many literary associations. Writers born in, living in, or visiting the city, have been inspired to write about Edinburgh's landscape, buildings and people. Most parts of the city can claim a literary connection, whether through the residence of a literary figure or a mention in a poem, novel, essay, journal or letter. Some writers have always lived in the city; others have studied in Edinburgh, eloped to Edinburgh, worked in Edinburgh, retired to Edinburgh. Many have had their work published by one of the city's many printing and publishing houses. Edinburgh has libraries and literary organisations; the Scott Monument, the tallest memorial in the world erected to a writer; The Writers' Museum, dedicated to the lives and works of Scottish writers; Makars' Court, a national literary commemoration; and the annual Edinburgh International Book Festival, which attracts writers, and readers, from all over the world.

The idea for a book of contemporary poetry grew out of the hugely successful exhibition 'A Mad God's Dream: The Story of Literary Edinburgh' held at the City Art Centre during the summer of 1997. The exhibition was organised to celebrate Edinburgh's rich literary heritage, to mark fifty years of the Scottish Centre of PEN, and to coincide with the International Congress of PEN (the international organisation of writers).

Beginning with the earliest recorded work, the late 6th century epic poem *Y Gododdin*, written in the celtic language which became modern Welsh, the exhibition highlighted key periods in Edinburgh's literary history, from the 16th century to the 20th century. Portraits, paintings, sculpture, original manuscripts, photographs and sound recordings were combined with quotations from selected writers, and included texts in Latin, French, Gaelic, Scots and English.

Edinburgh has maintained a central role in the development of Scottish literature. The mediaeval makars, arguably some of the greatest poets writing in Renaissance Europe, included William Dunbar (c.1460-1520), court poet to King James IV, who wrote of 'the bliss and glory/Of Edinburgh, the mirry toun'. By the late 18th century, Edinburgh was 'a hotbed of genius', centre of the Scottish Enlightenment, a golden age of cultural achievement, yet also a period of conscious effort to preserve national identity through the use of the Scots language. This is most noticeable in the work of Allan Ramsay (1686-1758), Robert Burns (1759-1796) and, in particular, Robert Fergusson (1750-1774), through whose poetry we have such a vivid view of life in the mid-18th century and who has influenced many poets down to the present day. His short life was crammed with creative energy, capturing the life of Edinburgh in all its rawness and vibrancy -

Auld Reikie! wale o' ilka town
That Scotland kens beneath the moon;
Whare couthy chiels at e'ening meet
Their bizzing craigs and mou's to weet:
And blythly gar auld Care gae bye
Wi' blinkit and wi' bleering eye

(from Auld Reikie by Robert Fergusson)

The 19th century witnessed the immense popularity of the poems and novels of Sir Walter Scott (1771-1832), for whom Edinburgh was 'Mine own romantic town'. Edinburgh also featured strongly in the work of Robert Louis Stevenson (1850-1894) who never forgot the city of his birth, his 'precipitous city' of 'draughty parallelograms' and 'meteorological purgatory'.

A new literary revival in the mid 20th century was led by Hugh MacDiarmid (1892-1978) and the literary circle which gathered in Milne's Bar and The Abbotsford, two city centre pubs -

...Edinburgh is a mad god's dream,
Fitful and dark,
Unseizable in Leith
And wildered by the Forth,
But irresistibly at last
Cleaving to sombre heights
Of passionate imagining
Til stonily,
From soaring battlements,
Earth eyes Eternity.

(from Edinburgh, Midnight by Hugh MacDiarmid)

In contemporary writing, Edinburgh continues to inspire a wide range of novels and poetry, yet:

'As a city, Edinburgh is a two-faced bitch'

(*Skinner's Rules* by Quentin Jardine, Headline Book Publishing, 1993)

It is a city of contrasts, a city where the past is inextricably entwined with the present, as it looks to the future.

With the beginning of a new millennium - and with a consciousness of the rapidly changing face of the city, its fast growing skyline, its growing and altering population - it seems the right time to record Edinburgh as it struggles to retain its character, while adapting to the demands and expectations of a modern capital.

Whatever the city means to people now, and whatever it will mean in the future, the timeless literary spirit will continue to inspire poets to write about Edinburgh.

'When Edinburgh has laid her hand upon a (person's) shoulder, the memory of that touch does not readily fade or be easily forgot'

(Lord Cameron in his address to the Edinburgh Sir Walter Scott Club, 1966)

Elaine Greig
The Writers' Museum

Great Junction Street by Jock McFadyen

Introduction

'Come on my muse! Reikie can you hear me?…
I ne'er cou'd part wi' thee, Reikie…'

Edinburgh has inspired both resident and visiting writers and artists through the centuries and remains an inspiration, as is evident in their work. There have been tributes to Edinburgh early in the last century in collections like *The Charm of Edinburgh*, ed. Alfred H. Hyatt in 1908 and *In Praise of Edinburgh*, ed. Rosaline Masson in 1912 in prose and verse. There was a flowering of anthologies in 1983 in *A Book of Old Edinburgh*, comp. by Eileen Dunlop and Anthony Kamm (based on early 19th century authors), *Edinburgh*, ed. Owen Dudley Edwards and Graham Richardson and *Edinburgh and the Borders: in Verse*, ed. Allan Massie. A gap has remained to date as there has been no anthology of poetry on Edinburgh by contemporary poets.

Poets are still moved to write about the city's contrasting images. This new poetry which reflects today's Edinburgh has been waiting to be collected and now appears in this volume. Our idea to compile this volume was facilitated by a Scottish Arts Council grant and made possible by the support and encouragement of The City of Edinburgh Council.

Since our call went out for contributions to this anthology, the response from poets has been tremendous. The poetry that has come has proved beyond doubt that Edinburgh's muse still works in mysterious ways and can continue to inspire poets to write about its protean quality, as it is always capable of surprising in a pleasant way. So we have poems which capture its charm, its beauty, its sadness, its people and the richness of life that it offers. The book has grown of its own accord, taking shape as the poems found a place for themselves. A thread was provided by the themes the poems deal with, yet each poem is unique. At the end of the day, the final choice was made with poems that fitted the kind of book we had envisioned, namely, ones which would, quite obviously, reflect Edinburgh or, in other words, ones in which Edinburgh was an 'actor' as it were. If there were too many poems on any one theme, we had to choose the one most suitable to the unifying thread that wove these diverse works of art together to justify that *Edinburgh* was, and remains, *an intimate city*.

This millennial volume is timed to celebrate Edinburgh's 'Awakening' to a new 'Freedom' to what seemed a dream carved on a headstone: 'Saorsa airson Alba' was realised, for 'at last we hae oor Parliament back'. But what does this freedom mean to the parliament on the pavement of the 'two men and a woman who sit arguing' in 'Nicolson Square' or to an 'auld man in the Cougate' with no hope of 'Foreign Aid'? Does it matter to the 'tramps and adulterers' who wait for a bus at '8 a.m. on a Sunday' at 'St. Andrew Square Bus Station', waiting to take them away from it while others lie smug in their beds, assured perhaps, of a secure life in Edinburgh?

The poetry shows how Edinburgh has evolved and how it appears to the artist today. It is no longer a city of 'fog belching from a hundred-thousand chimneys . . . blocking roads from cobbles to chimney tops . . . leaving you alone with your feet and your ears.'[1] It does, however, remain a city of 'garrulous stone', an 'old town' with '17th Century Buildings'[2] as a foreign visitor marvels, promising surprises - pleasant, stark, sad, but always with that intimacy which is peculiarly hers. 'Here new and old are as one'.

What makes a city a city? Its architecture? Its cityscape? Its changeable weather which defeats its cycle of seasons? What about the ghost cities in the world, abandoned by their people and now valued only as historical relics? Surely it is the life within a city which makes it a pulsating, experiential reality? It is its people - living, loving, despairing, hoping - who keep it alive - a vibrant reality that they and visitors to it can identify with or relate to.

What brought all these people here? Was it, 'need/or greed, compulsion, even hope'? Some, like 'an old friend who's never lived anywhere else', discovers that 'Here's gone. Elsewhere has arrived'[3] at his doorstep, some having come 'long ago', digging in their roots, having 'thrice married in Scotland'. Some meet one's eyes, they are 'peevish eyes' which 'apologize' for existing, perhaps never to be accepted until life's irony blends them in the city's earth, after an 'Edinburgh Funeral'. This is a city of 'such contrasts', in its people and its attitudes. One can 'choose to see' its many aspects, a city known for 'shopping, leisure, culture and

steeped in history'. In this volume we see this 'kaleidoscope' through its contemporary poetry.

This book offers a trip through Edinburgh. One can have the first glimpse of the city in a 'grey haar', or stare mouth open at sunset on the 'molten rock'. We are introduced to Patrick Geddes's much loved 'mony-layered tenement(s)'. to its 'wynds, the howffs', its 'grace, design' in 'stane', its 'cobble mile'. One can hear the sounds of the city as a 'pipe-band . . . strike(s) up a tune' on the High Street, ensnaring passers-by through 'pneumatic melodies'. And looking up one can see the fortress which keeps vigil over the city and its many processions, listening for 'The One O'Clock Gun' to boom without fail, wondering 'what party came first foot upon this rock?', sympathetic to a patriot who 'skailt a tear' recalling the past, hoping it will be written 'down . . . of a word'.

The past and the present crowd together in this city of 'Bards in the makkin, bards lang deid'. Memories of 'Burke and Hare await your final steps', but the present 'confronts' you in 'an over-coated figure' and one wonders, is it a suppressed 'dark half throwing away the mask of respectability for one night'' chasing 'illicit pleasure . . . down narrow closes'? But there is also the other past which remains preserved in 'the Card Catalogues of the Central Library', 'dignified and noble . . . typed or handwritten' alongside the 'channelled logic' of today's 'computerisation'. But walking out, one might hear 'the walled-up' dead's 'stifled cries' in a 'Close'. Yet, on turning and entering St. Giles Cathedral, one

---

1 Hugh Scott, 'Auld Reekie'

2 Alone Sekizenge, 'A City in the West'

3 Gael Turnbull, 'Lifetimes : Not Altogether Strangers'

can find solace in 'history and holiness hang(ing) together in subdued medieval splendour' or on 'Remembrance day morn', wonder if 'this is the way the warld ends . . . with a boke'?

But this is not just a city of phantasmagoria or without humour and hope. An adventurous climber on Edinburgh's 'Salisbury Crags' finds his dreams triggered off on recalling Bruce's spider, in an amusing parallel with his own predicament, suspended under Edinburgh's sky. And if one looks north from the Lawnmarket, the city offers a view over 'the narrow confines of the past'. The aspect is 'ever changing, /developing', allowing a soul to 'unravel, to soar' pulled by the 'magnetic north'. Yes, one can say to oneself, 'a'll away an get ma rollers oot /a've a feeling in ma bones that somethins roon the corner'. And even when 'night falls quickly' as office workers leave it on a 'Winter Night' 'this Metropolis' can be seen for miles . . . glowing orange like a prehistoric fire'. This 'Athens of the North' has always been 'the Toun' to those who have decided to meet in this intimate city.

The nostalgia is poignant while remembering the 'Lallans' meetings at the Abbotsford in the 'Forties . . . Fifties' or even in one 'old man' recalling his young bride as he watches the night end with a blackbird's song at 'Milne's Bar'.

The days lengthen and in 'Charlotte Square' garden 'are thousands of blue and yellow crocuses'. The light lingers and soon it is summer when the 'Festival's upon the Town'. 'In August the city grows, groans more, and weighs more' 'fraught with Festival fever'. 'Shoppers . . . jugglers . . . Big Issue vendors line the street' from Princes Street, up to the Mound. The city is 'alive with people all young all handing out leaflets to events which must not be missed'. Edinburgh's people mingle with this new wave of festive activity, and feel the mesmeric hold of street performers, 'spun' into participation 'following the drumbeats of a thousand years', brought to them at their doorstep by a dancer holding their 'trembling eye . . . in (a) ghostly stare'. And from this 'pale-as-ghost girl with flowing hair - wraith from another land' they have been known to gather 'in a mossgrown courtyard' in 'Tweeddale Court' to hear poets' 'voices', 'each poem unique, a small comet - complete'. But the voices have moved with time to the new premises of the Scottish Poetry Library further down the street.

Amidst the cityscape are its green lungs, where boyhood days are relived in one having 'kept up practice in the Meadows long after schooldays'. This is everybody's city. On an Autumn day 'widows, failing, independent' walk in 'Moray Place Gardens', 'their burden concealed' by 'the 'tinkling . . . from the collars of neatly-stepping dogs'. There are 'bairns at play, sober older citizens' who find freedom or retreats in 'Edinburgh's Botanics', 'this humanising scientific place'.

This city with its humanising aspect is home to 'gulls . . . geese . . . labradors' who haunt 'The Park', to 'laughing green woodpeckers' in its 'Hermitage of Braid', as the urban and the rural confront each other constantly in this city. Life continues in its wee confident creatures - in polite 'Boss gull' who steps aside saying "after you, squire", or the cheeky grey squirrel who pretends "I'm an innocent forager". We can feel sobered by 'Ma Pigeon' who explains that like her human counterparts in the city she is "after a contract from Special Uplifts" or murderous when 'a grey mouse' jumps out of a toaster jubilantly squeaking "tee hee hee, you'll never catch me!"

This city can evoke surrealist images in a semblance of life in the illusion of 'a swan' in 'a plastic bag' 'caught in a tree' or 'a beetle' in a window cleaner 'High on Eton Terrace' and bounce back to reality, spotting a spider caught in an artistic deluge 'between Paolozzi's bronze points'. But a visit to 'Edinburgh Zoo' makes one wonder, have we made this city our own 'cage', locked behind its 'bars', bearing it with the 'same long patience ' as the animals we keep tethered there?

This Scottish capital has its changeable weather. It can surprise the castle even as it 'display(s) its power in rounded battlement', coming in 'a storm-force' of sudden rain 'against' which 'there's no defence ...we just put up umbrellas', 'the dark blossomings of bobbing brollies'. Or on an April day 'some comical god cuts open a down pillow and shakes it over this city' and 'snowflakes tumble onto ...nodding tulips and fading daffodils'. But it can also have its memorable rare moments of an 'Edinburgh Solstice' when 'light throws its arms around the night, won't let it go' - that 'touch' which is a poet's 'inspiration'. Summer visitors are sensitive to 'a wine-chilled wind' blown 'down from Fife', the harbinger of rain. In an 'Autumn dawn', 'beyond' what was the 'Nor Loch', after the rain clears, there is, for Edinburgh's people, the reality of 'the ridge, this cityscape, their capital'. And what remains in the memory of anyone who goes away from it is its 'sharp northern light ...too precious, too clear' to forget.

This is a city of culture with 'bands ...parades, crowds, concerts, plays, gardens' and its many galleries - of modern art or of sculpture, the city of 'Dovit Hume' and Fergusson and Walter Scott. An older visitor can hope he can recall the freshness of a child's wonder as he wanders into the portals of 'the Gallery of Modern Art'.

It is a city of hope, which has seen many Hogmanays with its 'revelry', waiting for that moment when 'fireworks burst into life, cascading over the castle' and hear the intimacy of 'voices in unison' as people welcome one another to a 'Happy New Year' in Edinburgh. But this city is special. 'Wiv goat mer than wan language ...wur each ai us bitsae awthings ...an as lang as we remember tae celebrate that', Edinburgh will remain the intimate city it is.

It is a fun city with its rugby and football enthusiasts, as on many an afternoon 'the first supporters march down from London Road' and 'Easter Road basks in their dreams'. It nurtures many a dream - a lover's dream - encouraging a romantic to 'continue looking for' love in an 'Edinburgh of passionate spires and of declaration'. In its 'passion of Autumnal red when the Pentlands set their wine wind free' it can encourage a declaration of love calling the wanderer 'homeward' to 'stay' here forever.

Edinburgh has drawn visitors who search for its essence in its 'souvenir stores ...among teaspoons with castles ...teddy bears in tartans', caught in its commercialised display. This university town also attracts one-time students who haunt 'Buccleuch Place', remembering 'the streets of ...student days' in this city of 'Continuing Education', returning with their 'student daughters and their impecunious thirsty boyfriends ...float through Marchmont's genteel streets ...and feel out of it all'. For them 'there is only one human story: it ends in leaving'. Yet for some a return to Edinburgh can call for a celebration, enjoying 'drinking Camerons' and affirm 'what a delightful way to spend a holiday, getting merry, singing songs ...feeling' they 'belong ...more at home in this city full of strangers' with its sense of intimacy.

But all its visitors have not been ephemeral. 'There are three generations of Singhs now ...dressed in tartan'. And the city is filled with 'a heady aroma Chinese, Italian, Indian cuisine' which blends its ingredients to serve 'a piece de resistance in haggis pakora'. This is a tribute to the links of 'grandfathers from the Raj', a remnant in 'an ambassador car, an unlikely presence on Edinburgh streets' in this city of surprises.

This myriad life can be viewed from its many prominences. One 'can see Edinburgh cascade down to Leith, the Forth, Fife'. On 'one of those ice-blue days in January' one can gaze with misty vision 'across the Forth' . And after 'Scanning the Forth Bridge' one can saunter down to 'Granton' 'where the city trails off'. Or one can have a choice and walk along Portobello instead 'where the sky is blue and the sea is green', and stop to have 'ice cream' and build 'castles in the sand', metaphorical or otherwise, depending on one's age. And if one has taken the 'Edinburgh Bypass' to avoid 'road repairs ...queues ...sleeping policemen',

one can come back again - this time - from the 'Pentland side (of) brown bodhisattva ...overlooking the city that (one) love(s) ... of eightfloor tenements stacked with bright square lives'.
But all is not built up residential cluster here. There is an occasional 'unofficial breathing space' where 'nature the anarchist (still) runs riot'. 'Its days are numbered' however, as 'a hoarding's shadow' will announce 'the promise of luxury flats' since 'the city is tidying up loose ends'.

So is this city 'on the wane or continuing to grow?' It is 'imaged in the round of (a) startled eye, the song on (one's) lips, the beat of (one's) step, (of one's) heart' even when one is 'touring the globe'. It changes, but it is for its visitors, its people, its artists and poets a 'unique city which one cannot fail to love' because of its intimacy. It remains a haunting reality which one 'ne'er cou'd part wi'. 'Now is needed some act of imagination that brings all together, and this has been done'. This volume is a testimony to the perennial appeal of Scotland's capital.

Bashabi Fraser

The Enchanted Capital of Scotland by Jessie Marion King (1875 - 1949)

Edinburgh

I came to Edinburgh in a grey haar,
saw ravens dance down winter slate,
dribbled milk down my chin at dawn
on the frost of a dead volcano.

Saw sodium-filtered stars lick the red night
over the Opium Eater's gravestone.
Saw cobbles dance in the moon-glimmer,
gliskin under students, beggars, whores,
methsmen and schizoid dreamers.

Saw the wind whip the dresses
of calf-legged schoolgirls
while I throttled time in the Central Library,
shivering in starving sundowns.
I read dead poets then scarpered
down hungry closes.

Reekie, my mother's city and her mother's.
My parents married there,
amidst all the cremated ash
and garrulous stone of the place.
Ashes and bone of my people in dark mosaic
of wynd and sunless tenement.

(from Wolf Dream Alba)

Tom Bryan

The Awakening

I climb the springy turf to Arthur's Seat
And reflect, that beneath my feet
The fire's breath of the earth still surges below,
And rose to anger in this very place,
Twenty, thirty, forty millennia ago.

I look across to Edinburgh and remember, that as a child
I saw the honours of Scotland, tamed behind a wall of glass,
And Edinburgh bereft of pride, its throne laid bare,
But always had the quiet air
Of one who waited and hoped.

I watch the city now and sense its old heart stirring,
Its limbs flush with strength, that were tired and lame;
Edinburgh, our pride, the seat of our nation,
Ready to grasp the mace of governance again.

Julie P. McAnulty

Edinburgh from Arthur's Seat by Hugh William Williams (1773 - 1829)

Swearing In   for Jennie Renton

Sloughing off the chunky gansey of hickdom
knitted over twenty years of Highland life to discover
my city slicker frock coat was tight at the bum,
nippy round the waist, I was pleased to follow her
to the temporary substitute Parliament Building
where the Authentic Voice of Old Pulteney declared
today was the day for swearing in.

Immediately we determined to attend
and did all right, though we couldn't get in,
meeting all kinds, from Honest Johns to Party hoods,
beneath the statue of my old, sadly misunderstood
fellow galley slave, John Knox, his black arm raised
I thought, in a gesture of universal benediction. Bless him.

When she thanked the Leader of the Opposition
for assuming his unpopular but virtuous position
she was suddenly engulfed in his tsunami handshake.

The 1st Minister, nowhere to be seen,
could not therefore receive the collection of my verse
I hoped would inspire him in the difficult days ahead.

We tried a side door but a big lug denied us again.
It didn't matter. I was glad to be there, glad it was then.

So we slipped off, through closes and wynds
to dine like harvesters on dark red wine,
cheese and bread, and talk of writers and books
till she bought - in uniquely female celebration -
a floppy hat - to wave me off with at the station -
while all the time the lovely day went in and out of rain
and the people of Edinburgh went their usual ways
hailing cabs and washing windows, papering rooms
and hoisting bairns, while the whole country turned
on arms that were raised.
So fine it was at the centre, so good to be there
in Edinburgh on Wednesday, 12th May 1999.
Day One, Year Zero.

Robert Davidson

The Big Hooley   (1st July 1999)

In the Assembly Rooms thenight,
people want tae dance, an celebrate.
The hall swirls tae the Fish Band,
kilts, skirts, troosers, shorts,
even the odd ball gown
twirlin an birlin in time tae the music
lik a shoal turnin as wan
in the ocean's currents.

Ah've jist danced wi an MSP;
Hell, evrybuddy in the room huz,
an Ah'm thinkin ae auld Edinburgh
n'how aw the classes
yaised tae live'n work'n eat
cheek bi jowl,
crammed alang the spine ae the auld toon,

n'Ah think ae ma sons
n'the rest ae their generation
doon in the Gerdens
listnin tae Shirley Manson an Garbage
n'Ah know they'll be huvvin
jist as good a time as Ah um,
n'Ah know they can ceilidh
wi the best ae thum,

furr this country isnae wan culture,
ur class,
wurr no wan generation,
ur gender,
wiv goat merr than wan language,
an strings tae wur bow,
wur each ai us bitsae awthings,
wi as many moods'n aspects
as the weather,

an as lang as we remember
tae celebrate that,
wull be fine.

Nancy Somerville

Reikie, 2000

For Dunbar it was the mirry toun.
Fergusson cried it a canty hole
And like a keek o glore and heaven forbye.
Here Hume transformed human thocht
And gave bien denners tae his freens.
Clark Maxwell as a bairn at schule
Screivit a paper for the Royal Society.

For thae that hae the lugs tae hear
Thae splores, high jinks, high thochts
Still echo roon closes, wynds,
Howffs and new toun drawing rooms.
In oor ain time Garioch and Smith
Were guy sib to Fergusson himsel.
The sheer beauty o the place still lifts the hert,
A beauty which some hae done their best tae hash.

For there's muckle tae gar ye grue
In Auld Reikie and in aw Scotland thae days:
Puirtith, ignorance and hopelessness,
Shoddy biggins, ill health, early daith,
Amang the warst in Europe tae oor shame;
Cheek by jowl wi commercial greed,
Affluence, mobile phones and jaunts tae Bangkok,
Efter three hunner year o nae government or misgovernment

But noo there is a glisk o hope.
At last we hae oor Parliament back,
Reined in yet by Westminster,
But sune we'll ding thae traces doon.
Ower lang oor caws for equality and social justice
Hae fallen on deif and distant lugs.
Sune we shall bigg a new and fairer Scotland
Wi Reikie a real capital aince mair.

Paul Henderson Scott

Freedom

After night, Edinburgh is spiced with frost.
The morning's blue, so pale it's almost white,
The oval of the moon above
Frail as the face of an old woman.

And in among the pearl-carved pillars and the plinths
Of Princes Street, the homeless sleep;
Underneath the doorways and the stairs they curl
Like hedgehogs.

As the wind picks up they shift and dig
A little deeper in their blankets, and some wake up
And blink and stare as I pass by.

As if their voices too have turned to ice,
As if they have forgotten where they are,
They do not even ask for money, only stare
Away into the April air.

And as I go I wonder
If Scotland's freedom means a jot to them.
On this cold morning as they feel the empty gnaw
Of hunger, and the wind biting at their fingers and their faces
Like a dog.

Kenneth C Steven

Down and Outs No 36 by Ronald Rae

Nicolson Square

The girl's left hand keeps her coat shut, the other's
empty. She's standing in the middle of the street,
the traffic braking to a stop around her.
Hardly sixteen: bleached hair, bleached skin, fear.

The man she's with: badly healing cuts and anger
clenched into a face, pressed-in bruises
where the eyes should be.
She's telling him she's sorry, and being sworn at.

Nearby, a parliament of two men and a woman sits arguing
upon the pavement; they shout at her to grow up,
can't she? A taxi horn blares -
she doesn't move. It's raining.

I drop my 50p into the parliamentary cup, and walk past.
Behind me, the street shuts like a book, the place marked
just at the point where he hits her
in the mouth.

When I'm back this evening the story will have moved on:
there will be no girl, no man and no parliament
- only you and I
and everyone else, and the street around us growing darker
as the sun abandons it.

Ron Butlin

Foreign Aid

His e'en fixed forrit, shauchlin on his dowp,
I saw an auld man in the Cougate,
Legless fu' and happit in a lang, black coat,
Guid wool, weel tucked ablow his stern
As he gaed, fit first, backside neist
And oarin up the causey wi' his airms.
Wi' muckle care he pit his stick afore,
A compass in the high seas o' his mind,
An' like Columbus, kep his course aye til
                         the 'Trades',
Whaur he wid win the treasure o' a bed.

Black nicht it wis; the wind stuid fair for
                         hame
When by cam twa Samaritans,
Braw, dapper chiels wha howked him
By the oxters up agin a wa'
Syne gaed on, weel content,
But left our ancient loon
Bamboozled, beached;
Nae stick tae navigate,
Nae bum tae oar ashore,
Wi' tempests screichin his heid
Cliff taps frae hame abune
                         the gurly grun.

David Campbell

26

Photograph by Lloyd Smith

From City Inscape

Looking between smoke-blackened buildings,
I had an *illusion*, sun-lit cian-pink cliffs. Impossible.
I looked away. I looked again. It was still there -
a vast theatrical backdrop, but no insubstantial
curtain, no mirage. Rough-shod it arrived.
Earthed, the Crags, holding magmatic intrusions,
give notice of a long lodgement, and with
the sleeping carboniferous volcano, await the show
which history would provide. Geology,
the 'makar' provided for the fortress castle
that topped the black volcano whose
basalt plug broke the ice-flow about
the rock. The drive gouged out, channelled
deep, athwart both sides, leaving on high
the ridge. The native rock breaks through
the Castle's stone: and we are bonded
to our human past and to that past
beyond our kenning. Now is needed
some act of that imagination that brings all
together, and this has been done. Suddenly
it seemed it was there - a mediaeval bastion,
fortress, a round as for a defence, intruded

Photograph by Lloyd Smith

on Chambers Street, its curve taken up again
and again on floor after floor in a new great
edifice, till at the top look north and see
the Castle display its power in rounded
battlement, now echoed here. Empty
this building of the artefacts of our history
and still it speaks of Edinburgh. Inside
not confinement but a liberation of space
and light. The *illusion* is of forms
of such purity of line, bathed in light
of that high ceiling, suspended
as if they had no other function
than to transport the mind. Ascend
and corridors running the length
of the building, are visions of vennels,
wynds, closes, lifted by imagination
out of the particulars of stone.
Here new and old are as one. In those
who accept, the pulse of life beats stronger.

George Bruce

Walk an Edinburgh Street

On a breeze,
Catch the past.
A cobble mile
Of trodden path.

Feel its life
Course through
Your veins.

You'll never leave.
All will stay.

Helen Walker

High Street

Here is sort of in the middle: between
some sheer facade going up, and all those steps
plummeting down from the pend; or west, out past
the rock, the only skyline is the sky
while east you're seeing right the way out to sea -

the procession is late so here, to pass the time,
the pipe-band it's meant to be meeting strike up a tune
it's like with earphones in pump up the volume and
THUMP the THUMP bass THUMP drum's
            THUMP what? THUMP heart
THUMP beat, snazzy filigree of the snares
and the fingertips' pneumatic melodies -

Cut to Interior, a passing coach,
press Mute, and just the quiet camera motors

arrives the procession airs collide metallic
brass and as above et cetera
press Pause and eventually everyone gets the message
and out of somewhere in between the lilt
of a melodeon has squeezed its way in
and continues its little tune, regardless -

Ken Cockburn

Castles

some words
sit on a rock
like Edinburgh Castle

tourists of higher ground
reach it with one breath

but I go round
forget it's there
in the labyrinth of second hand
book shop bargains
until I listen to myself
saying anything to please

one day
I'm going to write down
an Edinburgh Castle
of a word

a word that keeps
its palace inside granite -
a word to quicken my breath
and give me sore legs

so that I can't say
justice or trust
without hard work

Robin Lindsay Wilson

Edinburgh Castle by Man Ray

I Skailt a Tear at Castle Waa's   (ane Enbro sang)

I skailt a tear at Castle waa's,
At Castle waa's, at Castle waa's,
I skailt a tear at Castle waa's,
For the Wallace memory.

And I am but a dowie lad,
A dowie lad, a dowie lad,
And I am but a dowie lad,
A dowie lad, but free.

O hark the skirl hear pibroch play,
Hear pibroch play, hear pibroch play,
O hark the skirl hear pibroch play
The tunes o victorie.

An wisna you a weir-man,
A weir-man, a weir-man,
An wisna you a weir-man
That focht sae bonnily.

There's nae kirkyaird abune yer banes,
Abune yer banes, abune yer banes,
There's nae kirkyaird abune yer banes,
Wha de'ed bi treacherie.

Tho in that breist dinged Alba's hert,
Dinged Alba's hert, dinged Alba's hert,
Tho in that breist dinged Alba's hert,
Hansel at Ellerslie.

Leeze me on that gowden heid,
That gowden heid, that gowden heid,
Leeze me on that gowden heid
Wha hung on gallows tree.

The Castle waa's be your heidstane,
Be your heidstane, be your heidstane,
The Castle waa's be your heidstane
Tae mynd eternally.

Sam Gilliland

Photograph by Lloyd Smith   © Historic Scotland

Clach-Chinn

Rud beag air falbh o ionad-losgaidh nam marbh
Ann an Warriston, Dùn Eideann,
'S ann a tha cladh
A chaidh o chleachdadh o chionn fhada

Agus, air a spreadhadh ann an geal ann
Air aon dhe na clachan-cinn
A tha seasamh fhathast air èiginn,
'S ann a tha: *Saorsa airson Alba.*

Headstone

A wee bit down from the crematorium
in Warriston, Edinburgh
there's a cemetery
long, since fallen into disuetude

and, sprayed in white
on one of the headstones,
barely standing,
(I quote): *Saorsa airson Alba.*

Rody Gorman

A Day Out at the Scottish Gallery of Modern Art

I sit and listen to the son tell the father
all about it.
The form. The way of the sculpture.
How it runs and builds itself, fresh
in his clear six year old mind.
I listen, try to reach back
to when, my eyes were new
and truly open.
I try, and maybe a glimpse
of what he can see.
Then it fades behind the mist
of time and habit.
Maybe though, he'll teach me again,
to look
and feel
again, before the mist
turns to fog.

Tom Murray

Armature

In the sculpture gallery,
opened two months,
a spider has webbed the spaces
between Paolozzi's bronze points.

It's the way things happen;
we intend, we make,
then the natural world amends, adapts,
goes its own sweet and random way.

Colin Will

Surrealism in Ainslie Place

From my window I saw a swan
Caught in a tree,
The wind stirring its feathers:
A plastic bag.

I saw the Water of Leith
Drifting with snow,
Thick and white:
Edinburgh effluent.

I saw a beetle,
Spiky and black,
High on Eton Terrace:
A window-cleaner.

I saw a ball,
Orange and huge,
Nudging Fettes College:
The moon sinking.

Nancy Macintyre

Moon and Meadows

The moon must have been there all the time
but only now did it turn its gaze
in his direction. As he picked up the ball
there it was, staring intently at him, ·
white-faced and serious, leaning over the sill
of prehistoric lava that at other moments
he would have said was the familiar silhouette
of Salisbury Crags, friendly and visible from home.

He'd kept up practice in the Meadows
long after schooldays. Walking now with the moon
like an extra football following him back,
he turned to the patch of grass where darkness
was closing in, and saw himself among the others,
only his shirt standing out in the dusk, reaching for the ball,
and felt himself confused between moment and memory.
Moon and Meadows, home and panic-strangeness swirled

as he recalled those names were forty years behind him,
but still was unsure which self or year he walked in now
with the moon accompanying him more sternly,
an escort to whom years were indifferent and
the volcanic Crags an intrusion it could ignore.
For a moment the moon and darkness were all that counted
- his familiar streets a shelter he could only faintly see,
their lights the torches of a rescue that might reach him yet.

Hugh Macpherson

The Meadows by Cathy Outram

Swithering on Salisbury Crags

Work or write? Ditchdull island
or glittering city? Looking
down, as much spider
as bard, dizzily dreamweaving
the ground I had to make up,
Salisbury Crags suddenly
became the gash
between necessity and a future
impractical as art.

Still, I am exiled to that
solidfrozen highlanding moment
when I took The Bruce's spider's plunge
on Salisbury's beautiful useless peat bank.

Kevin MacNeil

Sic itur ad astra

What party came first-foot upon this rock?
Let's keep it simple; make a plain surmise
and say a handsel for this vantage point
was marking sunset, sunrise and night sky;
consider it a day much like today
before a fire was seen, a posthole sunk,
a terrace cut or house wall woven here,
before a river's firth had flooded in,
before the woolly rhinos had passed north,
before a myth of gods or kings accrued,
before wild horse or giant elk were culled,
not really all that many years ago;
forget how various languages since passed
have worn away the memory like wind
yet filled the gaps with lesser stories. Ask.
Perhaps the ice, though largely gone, had left
a last cold pocket, shaded and tucked back
against the north wall of the crag-and-tail.
The soul that worked a way along the edge
through scrub of briar, juniper and birch
to face such bear or lynx as might have slept
up in the higher clefts: what skin was she?
what mind was brought? There's only one thing sure:
she stepped out on bare rock as on a moon,
thus from the top won clear view to furth lands
and watched sky darken towards *ard-na-said*
over where now kirks, steps, wynds and gift-shops
rise a while from parliament to castle;
a scramble up an incline of a tail
one step that day in short gait to the stars.

Colin Donati

Close

They are still here, the walled-up dead.
Their stifled cries, a tightness in the chest;
blood pounding in our ears,
their fists on doors.

This slum is under the street.
Above us, twelve or thirteen floors
rise like Babel into Edinburgh's night:
chandeliers, mirrors, portraits,
Scotland's history, sins of the fathers.

This was once a butcher's.
When they unblocked the close,
moist, damp air blew in,
and faded stains in the plaster
freshened and bloomed.

Those who came on Egypt's royal dead
uncorked a stoppered air,
catching a breath of spikenard or myrrh
before it sighed and was gone.

Stumbling over cobbles, our feet disturb
a whiff of byre - cow-dung
and sweetly, faintly, hay;
round the next corner,
brief, fragrant, unmistakable,
baking bread.

Anna Crowe

St. Giles: The High Kirk of Edinburgh

History and holiness
hang together
in subdued
medieval splendour

Laying careful
cornerstones for
tourists decoding
symbol and starlight in

This house of God
resting on a
prickly past
laudable laurels

Yet sailing
sedately through
tolerant waters
with her Gospel
of saving grace
wholly intact

Into a third
millennium
seething with
trauma and change

James Adams

Remembrance Sunday, St Giles

Remembrance day morn
And what wey shall we mind thaim aw?
Fer ower the New Toun strassen
And Reekie's thrawn auld banes
Blootered loons hae blattered
the stanes wi boke.

Ower the well-drilled squares,
The rank and file of serried terraces
And wheelin crescents;
Ower plotrif pends and vengfie vennels,
Claikin close heids and blearie back coorts,
They hae bokit thair lager an chips.

What wey shall we mind thaim aw?
Whae boked up lungs on mustard gas,
Whase slitten wames tuimed guts
ower dub an saun
What wey shall we mind thaim aw?
No wi poppies shed tae martial tunes

Or sermons fae meenisters in uniform,
No wi nurses doucelie mairchin
Or peacetime sodgers tummlin.
Na, like be mindit bi like insteid.
Man's self inflicted pain bi the same,
Boke wi boke, in seikness and in daith.

Sea maws fae the Bass
Redd the causies clean
And wi a craik of a Cougate crone
And an advocate's waggin pow
They little collogue wi sic troke
As the lave tae thair bairns they boke.

And this is the wey the warld ends
No wi a bang, but a boke.

John Murray

St. Giles by Rupert Cracknell

The Thinker on the Royal Mile - Welcome

Dovit Hume-
Mans' wee trauchlin bites
Wheeshed ye awa
The objection an delay
"Nuthin but sophistry an illusion."

A king lik stane, ye sit
Kennin the limits:
Faith an reason's end;
Philo, oor brither in speirins
Guide uz in the age
Whaur the cell an gene
The plant an the lift
Need the freedom
O speerit, thocht-an saul.

Andrew McNeil

Room with a View: Lawnmarket

Imprisoned here, I gaze out over
Time and space, from a high rocky ridge,
Searching, through the
Constraining mesh of
Routine captivity.

Squeezing from the narrow confines of the past,
Evading stone-faced sentinels,
Channelling my gaze onwards, drawn to
Magnetic north: over trees with yet
Unbudded branches
Reaching up in praise;
Lazy swathes of green,
Unaware of the promised new birth about to
Burst forth and
Shatter complacency; buildings on the
Fringe of a once-new town, ever changing,
Developing,
Jostling for space - to survive, to progress.

Breaking across my line of vision, a dense blue band
Highlights a distant kingdom, bathed in gold, with
Hints of bright-crowned peaks beyond.

Disruptive squalls, temporarily
Obliterate my direction, my still
Subconscious desire to
Unravel, to soar, to realise my, as yet,
Undiscovered self.

Eilidh MacGregor

The Hoose o Licht   praise-poem ti Patrick Geddes and his successors in Embro's cultural revival

We biggit a land:
A mony-layered tenement,
And as it rose, we scarcely kent
That sic a shooglie pile wad stand
The blufferts o the north. We feared
Fir murlie waas wi the bleck rot,
The clock's quick chaps.
           But then appeared
The traivelled fowk wha socht a hame,
Wha lairned us even as we lairned thaim.
Mithers fund rest there wi their weans
And sang the lines we'd lang forgot;
We walcomed chiels wi metal and pent,
Ti limn their legends i the stanes;
Sae wi the turn o a shair hand
They wove a spiral fae the sand.

We riggit oor space,
That we cuid constellate the years
O the lang mirk and the tentit base
Wi the words o oor ain and the warld's seers;
This is oor ootleuk touer: a guide
Fir the passin pilgrims ower the tide.

Tom Hubbard

Embro Toun

Salt on yer tail - she's a hotterin stew
O the kent, the fremmit, the auld, the new
The cassie-claik o the Embro hoors
Rikkin an rerr as Turkish flooers
Fur coat frills on a bare bumbee,
Is the show a stoater? Pye an see!
Clinkin thochts are a chinkin glaiss
Wit is gowd, an pretension's braisse
Dour an dozent, or sherp's a gleg
Are they takkin the rise? Are they pullin yer leg?
In howf, or close, or a wee stairheid
Bards in the makkin, bards lang deid
Shak doon wirds like a watter spoot
Idée fixe's a cloot wrung oot
Haive yer havers heich on the pyre
Gin ye'll nae thole heat - bide ooto the fire
Embro toun - yer a blacksmith's haimmer
Scotia's anvil - strike ye limmer!

Sheena Blackhall

The "One O'Clock Gun"

I cum frae guid Auld Reekie
Where ev'ry day at one
They fire from the Castle
A great big muckle gun.
And folks wi' clocks and watches
In every but and ben
Look up and check the time and say
It's one o'clock ye ken.

Chorus
One o'clock, one o'clock
In Edinburgh toon
The pigeons rise in Princes Street
And flutter roon and roon
While folk o'every nation
Go strollin up and doon
At one o'clock in Princes Street
In Edinburgh toon.

Noo tak a walk tae Holyrood
And tarry for a while
Walk along the Canongate
Or up the Royal Mile
There's Knox's house and auld St Giles
For ev'ryone tae see
But one o'clock in Princes Street
Is where you ought tae be.

Chorus

Ye canna miss oor Castle
It stands upon a Rock
And should ye hear a cuckoo
Its from the Floral Clock
Our Galleries and Monuments
Will fill ye wi' delight
But when the Gun goes off at One
Ye'll get an awfy fright.

Chorus

Dorothy Baxter

To the Card Catalogues of the City Library

Smooth-sliding drawers of blond wood, how many
Hundred thousand fingers have been crooked
Under your brass handles, have eased you out
And effortlessly pushed you shut again, flicked

Through your 5 by 3-inch record cards, and found
What they were looking for, or, better still,
What they were not? For decades now
Your cards, each anchored through a punch-hole,

Have slipped in their berths on the endless tides
Of wonder and enquiry. Years may have taken the edge
Off them, dogged their ears, desire and hope
May have marked them with enduring crease and smudge

But, heroic catalogues of the Scottish, Edinburgh
And Reference rooms, your day is not yet done,
You still remain, the working model of a memory
Built and driven by the energy of life, not of machine.

You are like Covenanters, dignified and noble even
In the unforgiving face of progress, a silent integration
Of belief and system. You are the sturdy remnant
That defies the channelled logic of computerisation.

Typed or handwritten, added to in different shades and styles,
Each entry is a backdoor key to somewhere else -
Dream kitchens on the grand-scale next to *biscuit-bakers*,
The Rhuvaig Smuggler lurking close to Barbour's *Bruce*.

There is, on the grubby screen of your on-line neighbour,
No sensuousness like yours, no random happy chance
In its literal hunt that can match the sheer delight
Of being ambushed in among your serried ranks.

The secret weapon of research is accident,
And you retain it in your finely crafted cabinets.
You are the polished morgues of unclaimed facts
And missing information. One day soon I expect

To pull out one of your gentle drawers, and find therein
A fragile, yellowed 5 by 3 by 14-inch, time-shrunk
Cadaver, with a card attached to one big toe that reads,
THE BODY OF AN UNKNOWN CITIZEN, PRESERVED IN INK.

James Robertson

Photograph by Lloyd Smith

Fergusson in Bedlam

I am Sir Precenter of the Pandemonium
     and the Cape; am I?
     Reikie, can you hear me, wha's me?
The Boreas blows, aye snelly, your stinking air;
I ken you, Reikie; your daft birkies, ranting fu;
the stairhead critics: whispering in the turnpikes;
aboun these waas: "the muse has gone frae him"

The torches blaze a' nicht down here,
     amang the regions of the dead, but
life's spunk's decayed, nae mair can blaze and
Reikie's wind sings sad music to the lugs;
     a' nicht, a' nicht
beneath the moon: black misery and shame,
that nouther carline-whores nor gowkies ken.

Come on my muse! Reikie can you hear me?
     I long to breathe the bliss of open sky; to close
my bleering eye, till dreams of comfort tend
my bed and wake to ane mair morn wi Phoebus...
     What sybil lead and left me here, where
     naked poets, amang burachs siccan to torture
     and to fleg the mind, hing their heads.

I ne'er cou'd part wi thee, Reikie;
     will you wi me? Ah, Reikie, it's business,
     weighty business I gie you; but when
the dead-deal taks me, will my wale o words,
like leaves, a' yellow, die; and you, waefu' as a
saulie, eithly tak tae your whunstane heart anither
scancing chiel; and pou his worth like a gowan?

Stuart B Campbell

56

Embro

Embro shall aye be pairt o me,
This citie biggit o muckle historie,
The stane, the grace, design,
The wynds, the howffs, makars
Forgin a unique identitie.

An identitie is whit it's aa aboot.

Weel I hae kent Smith, Grieve,
Broon, Bold, MacCaig, monie anither
Wi the crack in tawdry Milnes.....
Saturday nicht, aa there, the lauch....
Nips an pints till bang on ten,
Then the shout frae Bob .... The Baa's burst!

Bit anither baa wis aye found.
Pairties in hooses till the smaa oors....
Monie a cobbled street and wynd we toddled
Tae find oor repose.

Monie o those I hae kent
Are gane noo, bit still I find freens,
Anither generation o makars
Wha loo this ancient place.

We still dram, continue a tradition
O hospitalitie amangst the grey stane.

David Morrison

Milne's Bar by John Bellany

In Milne's Bar

The old man sits with his back to the wall;
staring and crinkled, he grips
his pint of light,
his hand dry as dead heather.
He sees a stranger, a girl
across the smoky room.
She smiles.
The old man fingers the ashtray.
His night gets longer
until a blackbird starts to sing.
His young bride beckons
from over a stream.
He almost gets up to go.

Jim C. Wilson

Lallans

At the Abbotsford, in Edinburgh's Rose Street -
famous, the locals said, for late-night whores -
the Lallans Makars often used to meet
within late 'Forties, early 'Fifties doors:
MacDiarmid, Goodsir Smith and Douglas Young,
myself, Scott, Garioch and, once, MacCaig,
discussing life or death for the Scots tongue,
sickened to dialect before the plague
of television, cinema, radio,
where English or American is spoken
with only poetry left to strike a blow
against a trend too strong now to be broken.
Raising his empty glass, Young cried: "Some mair!" -
the barman brought a pole and let in more air.

Maurice Lindsay

A Guid Hing Fae Calton Hill

Huv ye ever hid a guid hing?
Dae ye ken whit a guid hing is?
Weel, ye fling open yer windae,
plant yer eblows ower the ledge,
an hae a guid gowp oot.
Sometimes ye hae a wee keek furst,
an somethin catches yer eye, ken,
a guid fecht or a wean gettin battered,
an ye want tae hae a better gowk.
Ye need tae mind yer rollers but,
they aye catch oan the windae frame.
A like tae hae ma rollers in - jist in case.
The guid thing aboot a guid hing is,
ye can see whit's cumin up yer close, be prepared n that.
Like thae thievin salesmen - ye see them cumin.
"Missus, would you be interested in a set of encyclopedias?
Answers to all your questions?"
Answers tae aw ma questions? Who's he kiddin?
A'll no get answers fae a big fat book.
Mind A could get them fae thon wee fat cooncillor,
bit he only cums oot in May.
Naw, A widnae tak ma rollers oot fur him.
Bit don't start me wi thae politics.
Did ye hear aboot aw thae fowk stood up Calton Hill?
A wheen o fowk fae aw the pairts
o "Cool Caledonia" as they cried it.
Walked fae aw ower the place
tae build a wee cairn up the hill - richt up the tap.

A wee hing fae Scotland, like me at ma windae,
only they wur lookin doon on some
o thae sleekit weys at Westminster
Scunnert they ur. Cannae say A blame them.
Of course ye want tae keep yer ain schuils,
yer ain hospitals, yer railways. An watter - whit next?
A could fill a bucket on ma ain windae sill.
It's wur watter. Honestly the rnair ye think aboot it.
See if that wis me? I'd take a guid hing fur the last time -
Nae violence min bit A'd jist slam ma windae shut
an hae nae mair tae dae wi them
till they came roon tae ma weys o thinkin.
Enough's enough A say.
Excuse the aggression. A've aye been like this
an A didnae take that fae the wind.
A bit o the auld Pict in me yet eh?
A'll away an get ma rollers oot
A've a feeling in ma bones
that somethins roon the corner.
Or am A jist kiddin masel again?

Liz Niven

Calton Hill by Rodick Carmichael

Winter Night: Edinburgh

Night falls quickly as turning back a clock
but the City is alive with light.
Shops and cafes deny the darkness,
throw light at the street like baited hooks.
Offices empty workers onto pavements.
The yellow drip of lamps washes colour
from their faces as they pass beneath.
Cars, trapped in a magnetic flow, controlled
by coloured lights, thrust beams at the blackness.

It can be seen for miles, this Metropolis:
glowing orange like a prehistoric fire.

A M Forster

The Toun

Din Eidyn's days are long since done;
the name's as fanciful as *Camelot*.
Auld Reekie's had it too, her fires
fuelled by gas or anthracite, giving
only heat, no smoke, no light.

The Athens of the North? Aye, well,
maybe; depends on where you stand
but now you'd wait a long time
at the Cross to take some 'fifty men
of genius by the hand'.

Embra then? Sure enough,
it's been around a while
but how those west-coast Weegies
(two-syllabic, monotone)
fairly clip our size, our style.

Edin-burg! I heard that once
too often; a Yank in a car
who asked me for directions.
Keep right on, I said (a youthful prank)
and sent him to Dunbar.

Past names and present: a place
you think might never change. Stay
away too long and then come back
to find the grocery's
become an Internet cafe.

So, what's in a name? *Edinburgh*.
To me it always was *the Toun*.
I'll meet you up the Toun, I'd say,
the intention always clear
for could there be another one?

Jim Glen

Princes Street Seasons   for John and Doris Hughes

Narcissi needle through the grass
Across from Princes Street
French-knotted with embroiderer's art
They stitch themselves into my heart.

The Castle's taken off to sea
Upon a mass of foam
In Jenners now it's time for tea
I'm tired and going home.

With Scottish pound signs in their eyes
And plastic bags a-bulge
Sun-warmed shoppers fill the tills
Indulge, indulge, indulge!

The Festival's upon the Town
In jugglers' tights and Thespian gown
Up and down the skirling Mound
I think the whole world's to be found.

Big Issue vendors line the street
Papers flutter at their feet
A wine-chilled wind blows down from Fife
Exposing hungry, raw-boned life.

Valerie Hawkins

Princes Street

So soon after the rain
that the pavements glisten,
methodical pigeons pick at scraps

Unnoticed by them,
a grey squirrel scampers
light-footed across wet grass.

Her tail flicked in a wave behind
shoots invisible energy
into this Autumn dawn.

Jim Carruth

Edinburgh by Sara Ogilvie

Beyond the Nor Loch

We walk these paths below
the surface of the loch, watch as
ticking on the foreshore, that clock,
precise with flowers, counts away the loss.

Disgrace is on its hilltop, wars
are not. A cannon bawls the hour:
permission granted, class dispersed, leaves
floating with the jetsam they forgot.

Not anyone's but ours, this
paving crazed with footsteps,
making for the line and crossing it this time;
the ridge, this cityscape, their capital.

Brian Johnstone

Charlotte Square

Facing due east is the symmetrical façade
of St. George's Church, Adam's design
discarded yet harmonious, its coffered
dome imposing on Edinburgh's skyline.

It stands aloof from the traffic
encircling the Square, the din and fumes
where bedecked fillies once clopped. I jump back
as a souped-up motor-cycle zooms

too close for comfort. In the garden
are thousands of blue and yellow crocuses,
where Lord Cockburn stood to listen
to the comcrakes in the dewy grass.

Stewart Conn

Gàrradh Moray Place, an Dùn Eideann

Duilleagan dubha air an fheur,
fàileadh searbh na cloiche taise,
sop odhar de cheò
ga ìsleachadh mu na craobhan;
a' coimhead a-mach à bròn,
mòr-shùilean m' athar,
duilleag a' snìomh gu làr -
gluasad m' aigne.

Mun cuairt, coire thaighean drùidhteach,
comharra aois glòir-mhiannaich,
òrduighean cholbh clasaigeach
nach aithnich laigse san duine.

Gàrradh tathaichte aig bantraichean
fàilligeach, neo-eisimeileach,
a' coiseachd ann an cianalas an làithean,
an uallaichean ceilte.

Ach cluinnear an seo gliongartaich
coilearan chon grinn-cheumnach,
is chithear, fa chomhair nan taighean,
meanbh-dhuilleagan soilleir
gan leigeil sìos gu sèimh
aig a' bheithe chiùin, chuimir.

Moray Place Gardens, Edinburgh

Black leaves on the grass,
an acrid smell of damp stonework,
a wisp of ochre fog
lowering itself around the trees,
looking out from sorrow
my father's great eyes,
a leaf spinning to the ground -
the motion of my spirits.

All round, a cauldron of imposing houses,
sign of an ambitious age,
orders of classical columns
that do not countenance human frailty.

Gardens haunted by widows,
failing, independent,
walking in the wearisomeness of their days,
their burdens concealed.

But tinkling is heard here
from the collars of neatly-stepping dogs,
and against the houses
tiny bright leaves are seen
with the shapely birch tree
gently letting them go.

Meg Bateman

Edinburgh's Botanics

A humidifying scientific place, of well-marked plants
in linked glass houses. There's much bright water
and intelligent paths. Exotics reaching to the topmost
corners in from tropical forests and cacti

from many a desert place.

We are out to walk well-fed grass that curves around
bairns at play, sober older citizens
at their Sunday stroll beneath the old trees,
along the famous rhododendron walk surely unique

to this humanising scientific place.

And through a garden of heathers of all the world.
And the rock garden. Here basalts
from Giant's Causeway, conglomerates from Ben Ledi
and weathered stones from the old Bank of Scotland building

all set here with peaceful growing life.

Duncan Glen

Photograph by Lloyd Smith

The Park

one

we play in the park
the gulls the geese and labradors

my friend is training a pack of puppies
schoolparties are picnicking
air and earth sparkle with light

two

I walk through the park
the labradors the gulls and geese

people run, fly kites, play rounders
the mower cuts the grass in circles
all length and breadth of the afternoon

three

I wait in the park
the geese the labradors and gulls

now few remain as clouds amass
and one by one they all go home
as gusts of wind collapse the grass

Tessa Ransford

The Hermitage of Braid

a little oratory on the crag top
among the woods
a shelter-bed of rock

hangs out over the gorge
with the quiet tree-creepers
with the laughing green woodpeckers

perched in their morning
where the golden thread frays
on a thin wintry sunray

Valerie Gillies

The Alchemist's Art

Dark day in late November
A solitary figure struggles across the brow of the hill
Buffeted and exposed
And then, for a moment, stands stone still
An outcrop of flesh against the bleached sky

And as he moves off
The wind gives him wings
Black coat flapping on long fragile legs
He turns and merges with the jagged line of rock

Silent black lines transform themselves into screeching gulls
Wheeling round the blue and russet-red of Dumbiedykes blocks
And alighting on the moss-quilted roof-tops of Bakehouse Close
Clamouring for attention
Against the vast backdrop of rock

Mid-afternoon, and the last of the day's sun squeezed out
To spotlight the hill from the West
Glinting on outcrops
And transforming base rock into molten gold
The alchemist's art

Scene-change
Rock forged from fire and ash lies subdued
Trace of half moon hangs above
Shadowed by her companion darkness

A spilt ink sky runs down
To saturate the rock, soon stained black
And day-bold modern flats are quietened
And gently disappear.

Beverley Casebow

North Bridge and Salisbury Crags by Adam Bruce Thomson (1885 - 1976)

Embra's Hogmanay

It's Hogmanay!
And revelry
Is the order of the day!
Lager louts from all around-
North, South, East, West, come to town,
And at their best just make a mess
And at their worst will run you down,
On foot or in cars, as they gaze at the stars
Or the architecture, I'm not sure which.
But later in the dead of night
By which time they're completely tight,
On rubber legs, with unsound mind,
Inebriated bodies find
A close, some stairs or narrow wynd
Which leads to the Grassmarket.
A pleasant and lively hub of café society
By the warm, reassuring light of day,
A place to soak up ethnic culture,
Which by night is the coldly alluring domain
Of certain species of social vulture…
And the ancestors laugh with inordinate glee
To see the Sassanach turn and flee
Fae the *spooky* white heather,
The poofs, studs and leather
And the horrible, horrible weather.
It's only banter, the Tam O'Shanter,
But I am warning you here today
If in the Cowgate you should stray
After dark, it's safe to say,
Ghouls and witches who sleep by day
Will make you wish up town you'd stayed.

So! Sober up, and get a taxi
Back to your cosy B&B,
For if you go down all the way
Then who knows what the price may be?
With your body or your soul-
But you'll never leave here whole -
With your money or your mind
Everybody pays in kind.

Caroline Scott

A Moment in Time..

The clock is ticking,
streetlights flickering,
anticipation and laughter hang in the air.
People flocking from everywhere,
their teeth are chattering
and glasses shattering,
underneath the blue black skies
studded with stars.
Suddenly; splashes of silver and blue
fireworks burst into life,
cascading over Edinburgh Castle.
Then voices in unison
let out a cheer,
'Happy New Year!'

Christina Brown

Edinburgh   after Francis Thomson

It was one of those ice-blue days in January,
when the air's so pure you can read the lines
written for miles across the sky by jets,
when I saw the invisible and touched the intangible:

I caught an angel by the wing
as I lifted the post on my doormat.
It smacked the air like a startled pigeon
but I held fast - *Just tell me something before you go!*

So it told me of the fish that soars to find the ocean
and the eagle that dives to find the sky.
But I wanted something closer to home.
So it joked about the traffic on the ladder to heaven

that rises from Waverley Station. *Come on*, I said,
something important. But it escaped then
by distracting me, showing me from my window
the beams of light that cut the sky and fell

on nothing but the waves that walked across the Forth.

Allan Crosbie

Scanning the Forth Bridge

The bridge is wide. The Forth is deep.
Iambic trains are made for sleep.

Trochee trains are bright achievers,
sparkling through the cantilevers.

Dactylic trains cross the bridge very speedily,
passengers munching their sandwiches greedily.

All the girders and seagulls and Anapaest trains
can expect to get wet every time that it rains.

Spondee trains plod on, on, on, on.
Dusk, dawn, dusk, dawn, yawn, yawn. yawn, yawn.

Workers work all year round: pots of paint, nuts and bolts.
Cretic trains shake you up: nasty jars, sudden jolts.

The Amphibrach trains travel swiftly but rarely,
and say that the Dactyl's competing unfairly.

Of timid Pyrrhic trains
not one remains.

Robin Bell

Granton

Below the last outposts of architecture
is where the city trails off
runs out of steam
awed by the width of water
here unbridgeable
that has left flotsam and jetsam
two fat blue drums
a rope of brick houses
built for miners to spoon
coal from the ships
a garage a hotel
washed up, corroding,
But the pier is robust
as a backbone
it arches out of the mud
tilts upwind, upwater and prods
the coast with some of a bridge's confidence.

Ali Brown

Photograph by Lloyd Smith

Guid Auld Porty

Guid Auld Porty
By the sea
That's the place, the place for me
Where the sky is blue
And the sea is green (sort of)
Guid Auld Porty by the sea

Where the sand is supposed to be golden
And the sun shines bright
Many a time down the arcades
Have I spent on a Friday night
Guid Auld Porty by the sea

Eating your chips along the promenade
And your fizzy lemonade
The people so fair
And when the beach is packed in the summer
There's no place to put a deckchair

How I miss it now I've gone
To live in Leith
But my heart still longs for Porty
By the sea, in my heart underneath
Guid Auld Porty by the sea
That's the place I wanna be

Jimmy McCurdie

Portobello Granny's

When I was small I always loved to be
At Portobello Granny's
          by the sea.
Her tiny iron balcony above the Prom
Was a seat in the gods.
I sat there with the cooing pigeons
Above the Sunday people
And watched the walking fashion of the day from C & A
Lisle stocking legs
And frocks of crepe de chine
In sugar pink and helio and marina green
And three and elevenpenny hats
Go wafting past in a thirties' Show
          far down below,
And there was ice cream from Demarco
And castles on the sand
And seagulls like gents' handkerchiefs afloat upon the air
And a faraway boat beyond Inchkeith
          making for Leith
And along at the other end - the fun of a Fair.
The breeze blew very soft on me
At Portobello Granny's
          by the sea.

Last year I walked along the Prom...........
The old red sandstone tenement was gone.
The sea kept whispering
Inside its crawling silver folds,
A grey voile North Sea haar
          was hanging cold.

Betty McKellar

Edinburgh's Promise

for James W. Morrissey, in memoriam

Fog anchors me with tendril streams to grey walls
                from Grassmarket to Holyrood,
where slick cobbles pledge a twisted fall
                if I believe
that nothing underfoot wakens in flame.
                Let sleeping stones lie,
I pray, as my heart weaves me
                up and down High Street,
in and out of souvenir stores, searching -
                among teaspoons with castles
etched in their bowls, teddy bears in tartans,
                postcards of Highland cattle-

for your clan's name, a band of Celtic seamen
                who dropped anchor
five generations from Viking Waterford
                in the New World.
The clerk opens her cabinet, not guessing
                I come for attar of heart's-ease,
for healing in the black face of your death,
                that foothills
of ancient volcanoes can hold my flesh
                even as shadows
scumbling corners of rock facades
                can hold my tears.

She finds variants - *Morris, Morrison,*
    but not *Morrissey,*
wave after wave, your absence
    a dream within dream.
Escaping mist thickening to squall,
    daysavers bus ticket
as passport, I wander in blue pennons
    of lupine, their leaves
a soft green from Torphin to the Forth,
    where a tatting of Michaelmas daisies
fringes the road to a Leith café -
    a mug of white coffee,

cinnamon stick, sultana scone. A sea rainbow
    glides over the pier.
A tiny arc rives clouds, a thin rind of color
    grows a great sky grin,
as Edinburgh promises that you, dear friend,
    still smile at me, even in the rain.

Martha Modena Vertreace

Edinburgh Rain

A storm-force overwhelms the castle,
its white arrows drumming down
to soak the citizens and flood the town
as if to fill the Nor' Loch once again.
Against such rain there's no defence,
no bugle-call to tell us
SHUT THE GATES AND MAN THE GUNS,
MEET THESE INVADERS
WITH HIGH HEART AND CUNNING SENSE.
We just put up umbrellas,
They check the wetness
that invades the private neck
(deflecting it, no doubt, to someone else),
but they're no use
against the cloud-powered raiders
who fill up one's shoes
and saturate the pockets,
blot the spectacles and drench the knees
with raindrops bouncing like a plague of fleas
on the black glass of pavements.
Buses pass,
ploughing as ships do through the tide,
heaving aside a wake of water
over sodden feet
while the old gods of weather
laugh along Princes Street.

Alison Prince

April in Edinburgh

Some comical god cuts open a down pillow
and shakes it over this city.

Still whole snowflakes tumble
onto nodding tulips and fading daffodils.
American-style, the flakes are massive,
wonderfully vulgar with their bold showiness,
declarations of determined distinction.

Yet it is rare that Lake Michigan gives Chicago
what the Firth gives Edinburgh today:
a post-Easter surprise,
fleetingly beautifying the urban filth,
in this mild clime of iceless winters and sunless summers,
a sight temporary enough to admire
against the dark blossomings of bobbing brollies.

Hannah Ekberg

At Edinburgh Zoo

We make such tut-tuttings about zoos:
"The poor things given no space",
Every move, waking or sleeping, seen
By prying eyes, by these voyeurs
Who dare not look at themselves.

Most of the "poor things" are unaware
Of concepts like "freedom"
Which makes it so remarkable
As they peer out through their bars
At "*homo sapiens*, late 20th century"
That this variable creature, man,
Makes his own cage and
Then squats in the filth of it
With the same long patience
He pities at the others' zoo.

Hamish Brown

Small Game in Edinburgh Central

A gray mouse jumped out of my toaster -
three sleek inches, plus insolent little tail,
As he jinked off behind the Sugar Puffs,
I cried, "I'll get you, bastard!"
Reached for my biggest knife. He squeaked in riposte:
"tee hee hee... you'll never catch me!"

At six a.m. I potter out for my paper.
Boss gull's on the doorstep, jabbing at a binbag.
Backs to the middle of Spittal Street, rasps, "After
you, squire..." Shrugs his black-wings, casually
casts a look round for rivals, over his shoulder..
"You all right then? We're running this street now.
See me right, we'll look after you.
OK?"

Passing the Links, I spot a grey squirrel
hoppiting hither and thither, much like
the hero of a demented Game Boy game.
I shout out, 'Some sensible places, people eat
rats with bushy tails like you.' He pipes back:
'Mistaken identity, mate. Me, I'm an innocent
forager. It's those red shites need cooking,
if you can find one nowadays - har, har, har.'

Disconcerted, I turn to my old friend Ma Pigeon
whose extended family graze Bread Street all day
much like archaeologists digging for Homeric
shards, and three thousand year old grains of barley.
"Don't worry, son," she responds. "See us - we're stable.
Shower us with carry-outs, we'll cope.
We're after a contract from Special Uplifts.
Excuse, please. I must just collect
that stray peanut."

I am sure that not far, in Morningside and Dean,
urban foxes lurk, smirking. Edinburgh Central should be declared
a Game Park, and our new Parliament
should debate giving all fellow creatures the vote.
The gulls, I'm sure, support Rangers. As for the others,
Hibees or Jamboes, I don't care, they're us.
Me, I'm hereditary Dundee United
Wishing that cormorants too could flock to town.

Angus Calder

Easter Road

Easter Road rising to the Crags,
the wind from the Forth cold on my back
hustling sparse leaves
towards the football ground
like early Hibs supporters. Stands; taut green strands
angular arms entwined
leaning outward listening
for the crowd roar that will reverberate
round the curved corner windows of tenements
gardens and drying greens
reaching the rocketing church spire
and Abbeymount Techbase.
Now in the afternoon sun
shops spill out lush plums, red cabbage,
glossy peppers, warm blast of beer-laden air,
Ayrshire potatoes, hot pies, used clothes
second hand books.
The first supporters march down from London Road.
Easter Road basks in their dreams.

Elspeth Brown

St. Andrew Square Bus Station

8 a.m., a Sunday. I, tramps and adulterers
wait for a bus as if it were the Second Coming -
Stalin would have envied such devoid and concrete places
dedicated to a Saint whose sanctity
was bought by his unworthiness.
We are surrounded by litter, which
we try not to see similes in.

S B Kelly

Literary Gothic

The broken earth at Arthur's Seat exposes the city's stone soul.
The iron railings and tangled vines capture the last moments
of the winter sun over the Old Town. This is the perfect
setting for a horror story. Blend the rattle of bones with ink,
grind blood into the paper fibres and you have a best-seller.

As you turn the pages, footsteps follow you up empty streets
and each turn is a dead-end. The pound of your heartbeat
is deafening as night pulls in its wings and the fog slithers
down onto the High Street. You are no longer alone as ghosts
rise and stand pale among the rows of black-faced houses.

Hyde and Begbie lurk together in a shadowed doorway. Burke
and Hare await your final steps. Rebus is warm in a lock-in
at the Ox and no help to you. An over-coated figure confronts you.
Or is it your dark half throwing away the mask of respectability
for one night, to roam the streets in search of illicit pleasures?

Whisky burns your throat as you wait for the next victim.
You secretly delight in the fate of the weak, caught in the city's
icy tentacles. You share the sensuous thrill of the chase down
narrow closes and taste the bitter defeat of the villain's capture.
And in the last chapter when the loose ends are gathered together,

you slip away like an unsuspected thief from the scene of the crime.

Gerry Stewart

Edinburgh Solstice

Midsummer cloud forms inky bars
and sculptures,
peddled loaves and buns, purple
against the blue of midnight sky.
This northern, all-light sky.

My friend says - can I escort you
to the bar? - inclines his elbow.
I take his arm.
Inside, the Australian talks
of Ayer's rock and outback,
others talk of Ezra Pound,
the cricket score and -
my friend's brother appears and
whisks him from me.
Time for him to go.

What's your inspiration? someone asks.
Language, says one.
The land, I say.
The sky pebbles and smears
light. It licks along the streets.
Touch, I should have said.
My friend was whisked away.

Those bun bunches in the sky -
lamps of purple ink
are grapes of light - no,
gaps I cannot fill.
I gulp darkness on the slopes
of street.
Touch, I should have said.
Belonging.
Come back clouds,
light throws its arms around
the night,
won't let it go.
Lucky night.
Blessed - by proximity of
light.

Morelle Smith

Passing Through

Through subtle summer twilight,
the ambiguous dusk of another town,
walking with my student daughters
and their impecunious thirsty boyfriends
going slowly home from the pub -
tasting again real ale in pints -
I float through Marchmont's genteel streets,
see children's toys abandoned behind hedges,
families brightly windowed in well-proportioned
rooms - and feel out of it all.

Merely passing through, I kiss my goodbyes
and shake young lusty hands -
letting my soft-lipped daughters go -
while a black dog barks and barks
behind its railings, snarling at intruders.

Ken Morrice

Edinburgh

Yesterday, or rather last night,
I went to Edinburgh:
got a hangover, but I enjoyed
drinking Camerons and eating salted peanuts.

Where will I go today?
Not back to Leeds, that's for sure,
It no longer exists,
(Only in the cry of a seagull...)

Maybe the Forth Bridge?
Or the cottage at Dunglass?
Maybe the Royal Mile?
Or the Festival at last?

What a delightful way to spend a holiday,
Getting merry, singing songs,
Eating fish and chips, feeling I belong;
More at home in this city full of strangers,

than I am in Leeds.

Angela S. Hopkins Hart

August, Edinburgh

In Princes Street throngs, Edinburgh
He said, eyebrows up, "Pardonez moi ?"
To my "Where is Castle Street ?".
Of course with, Please and Excuse me.

Bands, jugglers, parades, crowds,
concerts, plays, galleries and gardens.
The whole thing an organised free for all,
a carnival,
more informally dressed than the Festival.

And another thing, In August the city grows,
groans more, and weighs more. It shows.
Bus stops, taxi stances, sprout linguists endlessly
who all speak a common language called
Waverley.

Face Painting to look like a Cree or a cat.
Singing blues, jazz, opera, pop, Gregorian
chants, celtic haunting melodies and then
bagpipes in the streets. An aluminium seat

at a Canongate cafe. Harmonies of coffees.
Different harmonies for visitors. As for us,
it take us out of ingratiation, out of isolation
to beckoning spaces beyond Kailyerd kitsch.

A song of Scotland to the world.
An antisyzygy counter symphony.

Neil mac Neil

Untitled by Aidan Bremner

Edinburgh Waft

There's something about that day.
It wasn't her lace shirt flapping
nor her pre-Raphaelite
red hair
tearing
down.

or

the fact that she
held Edinburgh's eye among
Bungee jumpers and birling jesters

or

the way she spun
her shawl following
the drum beats down
a thousand years

or

the winds of passing busses
flinging her hair into strange
looks of passers by

or

jugglers spinning
sticks of fire reflected
in her eyes

it was when she
held my trembling eye
in her ghostly stare.

Des Dillon

Tweeddale Court

At these summer gatherings
on August afternoons
in a mossgrown courtyard
with overhead a hanging balcony,
time could be centuries ago...

Strange music,
slow and measured dancing
from the pale-as-ghost girl
with flowing hair -
wraith from another land,
an existence of dreams.

And then the scrape and shuffle
of chairs being re-arranged
brings us back
to muted sound of traffic,
an unseen bustle of people
on the High Street.

Afterwards voices
flutter in the wind,
laugh in the rain,
sing in the sunshine.
Voices with things to say
each poem unique,
a small comet - complete

Travellers,
heading through the narrow archway
for somewhere other,
hesitate before they hurry past
sensing something exceptional.

Margaret Gillies Brown

After reading at the Book Festival

It's a short step from my shore
To the hyperventilating city,
Fraught with Festival fever.

No matter in which direction I walk
I'm always going against the flow.

Siùsaidh NicNèill

After the Festival

Going away, our habits, concerns
are thrown into yesterday
like the road lengthening behind:
before us sunshine, a clear sky.

Looking forward, we overestimate
this loosening of the life from the day.

Edinburgh in the Festival
alive with people all young
all handing out leaflets
to events which must not be missed.

We miss them. We see only
what we have waited to see
we do only the things
we have long planned to do.

Round us the city rises
brilliant through showers
sun striking on stone.

In this new place
we manage to keep at bay
the thought of coming back.

Sky massing clouds
car smooth on the road
the ache of tomorrow blurred
like the first stirring of pain.
Edinburgh dissolving behind
past coalescing with future
our only aim now to pretend
or perhaps to admit
no difference has been made
by our going away.

Moira Forsyth

Writing Poetry at Edinburgh Airport

Li Po said, 'To read poems is to be alive twice.'
At the airport it is easier to see how everyone is equal.
There is only one human story: it ends in leaving.

David Keefe

My Father, from this Bus

Come Sundays
only the castlerock
    is assured of its integrity:
other stones (shorn of bureaucratic attention)
    are full of self-doubt
      make pigeons fidget and crap.

From the bus circling St. Andrew's Square,
I can see Edinburgh cascade down
to Leith   the Forth   Fife.
My father, stepping from the pavement,
tilted to the wind,
is halfway to the sky -
a hand pinning his hat
an arm waving brave and strong:
the Old Master dismissive
of all, but his departing son.

He is one-time steward of my little freedoms
self-made master of all my lies,
yet only now do I see his silent reasoning
as, holding back the evening sky's grim heraldry,
he stakes his love amongst all the emptinesses
I have known and still must know

and, as the bus careers along Gorgeous George Street,
I settle back in my seat:
like the thin crowd shuffling into dark St. John's,
I cradle hosannahs for a father's hopeless love.

Tom Pow

Edinburgh Funeral   in memory of Mary Thomas

Looking down on the church's roof
from another dear friend's eyrie flat
I never knew how embroidered and sanctified
this wide nave and chancel hid
now filling, and filling, and filling
with her dark-coated friends.
Many have walked here from Marchmont,
Morningside and Toll Cross,
others driven from Oxford, Aberfeldy,
Yorkshire, London, Aberdeen,
or flown from Orkney. Her man
one of the very first people in Scotland
to become my acquaintance and friend,
many, so many years ago,
and she, for whom we are all assembled,
having come from Yorkshire, long ago,
thrice married in Scotland.
It could only be here, in Edinburgh,
       "and by Mary's wish,
         you are all to have a jar
         in the pub beside the church,
         "and to raise your glasses to her -
         I want her to hear!"
And how embroidered and sanctified
patterned and interwoven
the lives of Edinburgh are,
divided in liveliness and argument,
united in friendship, death and grief.

Sally Evans

Looking for Something I've Lost

In the Edinburgh of the early eighties I was in love
And climbed the hilly streets and waited in bright cafes, all for him.
I saw Edinburgh: followed its fingers to gain one sight of him,
Prowled streets to see the lighted window of his room

I have been in love since the eighties
Though it has been love I have not voiced
For with ageing I am wary of declaring myself
And so Edinburgh, the Edinburgh of passionate spires and of declaration
Is lost to me. Distant and still enchanting,
It is a drum to be beaten by others. The rain-swept streets of the city
With passages of light like wakes of ships are for other hearts to occupy.

Should I return to live there,
Alone? What community is there? It is a city for the young or for the settled
Not for the in-between .... A charismatic spectacle.....
And taunted always by another drum, tum-ti-tum-ti-tum,
.... Success played by plate-glass marchers lucky for a while....

Towns elsewhere demand less grandeur of the spirit. Like queens
Who have retreated and moved their armies of bruised nerves through the night
And become ordinary, they are restful places.

A city of flamboyance demands
I rush out to meet with those coincidences that sweep you off your feet,
Make you believe you live within a grand mechanical toy,
A snowscene you turn upside down and shake
And happiness tumbles down in swirling snowflakes upon a fairyland of top-floor flats
And closes leading up to revelations of the heart.

Perhaps, it is illusion I have lost, most of all:
A cartoon figure's freedom of a skyline.
Step after step, I have come down from giddy heights
As if, I'd thought of myself, as a Queen. Surely, Edinburgh can remain
Dream-capped, perilous, precipitous, attractive
On a scale worth admiring but not always matching?

There is no guarantee amongst the glitter of Edinburgh and its columns of wealth
Of finding love but a wise woman may still look upwards
Not let her own silence, her middle years, defeat her
Or rob her of Edinburgh's favourite goddess (she is in this room now) - Venus.

Maureen Sangster

Always..

In the winter of wedding white
When the Castle catches furtive flakes through history
And robins bounce in sight
Hurl your ski-boards down the slope
                    and walk with me.

In the dreamy days of drifting fog
When the Meadows' green horizon melts in mystery
Around the lost, whining dog
Rein in your steed, halt in your tracks
                    and stand by me.

In the afterglow of sunset
When the Forth reaches lazily to greet the sea
And seagulls drift home spent
Turn your yacht, touch prow to shore
                    and come to me.

In the passion of autumnal red
When the Pentlands set their wine wind free
And sheep stand in the gorse amazed
Whirl your steering wheel to veer homeward
                    and stay with me.

Bashabi Fraser

You Walk Edinburgh, Evening

You walk Edinburgh, evening
Dims the grey, light and wet
The sleek moist bricks drip
And dark are houses; silent,
City of a soul imploded,
Dreams of nothing. Creak-
Booted, old torn a man
Stands, unwanted, stick, no-noised,
Plunged in revulsion of
Own cheek - stubbled, red-veined.
Alone, eyes contact yours
And peevish eyes apologize
For existing.

Tim Cloudsley

Edinburgh Life

Edinburgh has such contrasts, if you choose to see.
Shopping, leisure, culture and steeped in history.
The castle stands impervious to the march of time,
It is almost as though it's watching the city all the time.

Shop windows glitter beckoning customers to come inside,
Their choice of merchandise is offered with such pride.
But to stand on a street corner buskers and beggars appear,
Which makes one realise life's choices aren't always clear.

Victoria Foster

Blending In

in recognition of 50 years for the Singh family in Edinburgh

Edinburgh was a cold host half a century ago
for the tailor from Amritsar; a grey place
for a Sikh who had looked on a golden temple.

There are three generations of Singhs now
to stir warmth into this stern outpost:
twenty families listed in the phone directory.

Dressed in tartan, they all assemble
to celebrate their several identities; a unique
blend of Sikh and Scottish cultures.

The spread prepared has a heady aroma
Chinese, Italian, Indian cuisine
with a *pièce de résistance* in haggis pakora.

They line up for the family photo, swathed
in their new tartan. The kilt looks good on them
and the twist of matching tartan in their turbans.

What would the old man have made of this,
the tailor? Would he have laughed or cried
or criticised the weave, the stitching?

He would have seen the colours of beloved flags
in a sway of pleats: green, gold, blue, orange
hot hues of India, of the Punjab, disciplined

to the Campbell tartan - the one in which
Sikh regiments marched curtly to the tune
of British monarchs. A second glance down

the Singh column in the phone directory reveals
new city threads to blend in: a swatch of names,
of new histories to tartan Edinburgh.

Christine De Luca

Photograph by Bashabi Fraser

Namaskar, Sir Walter   (in memory of my *Dadus*: Rai Sahib S N Chatterjee and Sri P N Mukherjee)

Namaskar, Sir Walter, I bring greetings from both my *Dadus*,
grandfathers from the Raj, retired pushers of fountain pens,
whose grand and innocent dreams you fed and fired.

My *Dadus*, paternal and maternal, I distinguished between them.
One was my Timarpur *Dadu*, blind but knowing every tree and pothole
of the dusty Old Delhi neighbourhood where unneighbourly Timur
once pitched his city of tents and where later conquerors built offices
which were, he said, the new temples that fed our stomachs.
My grizzle-haired bespectacled Mussoorie Dadu, lived evergreen
in the hills and each summer I would visit him in his 'English' cottage
with its rambling rose briars. I would visit all his neighbours too,
but go most often to the childless major whose Scottish wife
lured us children with her doughnuts, tartans and apple cheeks.

No two *Dadus* were so unlike, but your brave words lit up their shelves;
they roamed with you in the craggy Highlands, the buzzing Borders,
the great castles and, of course, the regal streets of Edinburgh.

Courteous Timarpur *Dadu* had worked in Defence and earned a title.
My sister sampled his sacred snuff on his four poster bed and I blew horns
and ruffled his snowy hair, pronouncing him 'a lovely boy'- my Ivanhoe.
He had all the *Waverley* novels - his sons grew up on their swashbuckle.
My sister, cousins and I would stroke the fading embossed gold,
turn the yellow termite-nibbled pages, and Timarpur was transformed.
We roamed with you in the craggy Highlands, the buzzing Borders,
the great castles and, of course, the regal streets of Edinburgh.

Mussoorie *Dadu*, blunt and restless, took me rambling on long walks.
He wielded his walking stick like some antique sword. His tongue too
was a blade: heavy and damaging at times like an old broadsword
or darting light with rapier thrusts, but always sharp and sparkling.

His dogged brilliance in Income Tax had won his rulers' grudging respect.
A juggler with numbers and words, he had your prodigious memory,
your love of books and travel and history. He gave me poems of passion
and adventure - a free soul, my wild Gallic Rover, my young Lochinvar.

Having roamed with you in the craggy Highlands, the buzzing Borders,
the great castles and, of course, the regal streets of Edinburgh,
I stand at last before your statue. *Namaskar*, Sir Walter,
from the bottom of my heart. Please accept these Indian greetings.

Debjani Chatterjee

Photograph by Lloyd Smith

Continuing Education

Buccleuch Place, 2000. The cobbles glisten
with memories of high heels flashing
along the streets of my student days
when we all wore duffel coats and
seamed stockings and straight skirts
and heads held high as high and
hair flying in the breezy wind.
It must have been cold but
we didn't feel it although we didn't
have thermal vests or any vests at all
and our thoughts were all of dances and
the lecturer in the polo-necked jumper
who talked about D H Lawrence.

The wind doesn't notice my hair is grey now
and even I forget and I even forget my bad knee
and the ankle that makes walking difficult.
I hurry into number 9 and there are my friends
with ideas tumbling over each other and
our tutor is waiting, smiling, ready to begin.
A glimpse of Edinburgh sun lands
on my notebook, and there's an untrodden-snow
sparkle on my new page.

Christine Lloyd

Man Reading by William McCance (1894 - 1970)

Ambassador

A friend
   who hoards

histories of
   Calcutta

in stories
   stored in

unpublished
   silos, spots

an Ambassador
   car,

an unlikely
   presence

on Edinburgh
   streets

Scotland
   had never

before seen
   one

of its kind -
   its polite

Indian chassis.
   My own

desire
   to inhabit

its shell,
   its Bengali

carriage -
   affectionate,

gentle,
   rounded

and
   serene -

is to do with
   memories

of family
   and space -

mobile and
   expansive.

But what
   drew us

to its
    strength

and steel
    was its

unmolten
    wickedness,

its couched
    ambition

it quietly
    contained.

The body's
    reflection

in this sharp
    northern

light was too
    precious,

too clear
    for comfort.

The only
    respite -

untold tales
    recorded

in its
    unwarmed

motor,
    one that

now spills -
    imagined,

dreamt,
    gradually

unveiling
    its

uncoiled
    secrets

in high octane
    elasticity.

Sudeep Sen

Edinburgh Bypass Blues   (Acknowledgements to William Empson)

Good morning   fasten your seat belts front and back
Thank you for not smoking   hold on tight
Drive safely   watch your speed   keep your distance·   slow down
    Slowly the poison...

Road repairs   queues likely   delays possible after Dreghorn
Low bridge   road narrows   smile please   round the bend
Remember mirror signals manoevre   keep moving
    Slowly the poison the whole blood stream ...

Apologies no animals   no invalid carriages   no men with beards
No surrender   no joking   no flashing except between consenting policemen
No waiting   no loading   politely please   tickets and regulations
    Slowly the poison the whole blood stream fills.

Sleeping policemen   traffic calming   no snoring   bumps!
Road narrows   keep your distance   potholers emerging   merge in turn
Beware low flying owls   don't look now   diversion via Joppa
    The waste remains...

Give way to slow moving swans   harpists this way   follow Leith
Heavy plant crossing   keep your distance   keep your hair on
Keep your pecker up   eyes on the ball   no shillyshallying
    The waste remains, the waste remains...

No entry   closed to highminded vehicles   keep up with the Joneses
Push your product   watch out for greenhouse effects   beware falling towers
Belt up   get knotted   buckle down   feel free   take a break
    The waste remains, the waste remains and kills.

Avoid rainbows   great crested grebe alert   danger trainspotting in progress
Caution holes in ozone layer   remember the fallen   report to Clarence
Smile please   wild fancies crossing roads   remember   remember -
        Frustration kills!
        End of restrictions   apologies for any inconvenience.
        Slowly the poison the whole blood stream fills.
        The waste remains, the waste remains and kills.

Martin Bates

Photograph by Lloyd Smith

Caerketton Hill

Inhale

Out of the coil the bypass roar
is sudden. But the other, Pentland side
is brown bodhisattva, breathing
shallowly. There's no flinch under
snowfall, no battening down and
firing up as in our thin tenements.
The snow sneaks into old farming furrows
fills the gaps between new shoots of heather.

Inhale

Pick up a red stone sharp in its
skin of ice. Before doing what
all people do, feel it in your palm
a tiny fraction of what it came from.
It's all that you can handle. Then
cranny it into the cairn, overlooking
the city that you love. In the hope
that the stone will remember you
down there. In the hope that in the city
you will remember Caerketton.

Inhale

Your big boots clip heather roots
necks already broken by the ice.
Hit the ground. Lift away the ground.
There are fossils of snow and mud in
the grips. But feel the unshakeable mass
under the turf.

Inhale

You can smell the sea, and the
mulchyness of hill water. But see
equally the urine fug away over Cockenzie.
The city's growing, a lichen on the Forth's
branch. Or, at night, a livid fungus,
a lurid haary all-loving Hogmanay kiss.

Inhale

Arthur's Seat's a wee blackhead plook.
The Crags a frown over the nearness of
the North Sea. And there are
eightfloor tenements stacked with bright square
lives. Oxygen bars and Sellers of Wine and Tea.
A need, still, for steeplejacks.
Tiny city. Tardis city.

Jennifer Hadfield

Edinburgh Gap Site

As you pass, the break in the terrace
widens, from a slit of random botany
to a chunk of sky with nibbled edges
between cold-shouldering gables,
an unofficial breathing space...

Nature the anarchist runs riot,
weeds flourish, sorrel, dandelion,
and every summer wild foxglove
bursts into brief glory. Honey bees
amble by, as if visiting friends.

Someday they'll dance to another
rhythm, when a hoarding's shadow
falls across this orphaned patch,
to announce its days are numbered
with the promise of luxury flats.

The City is tidying up loose ends,
planners are rectifying oversights,
the plot is ripe for development -
Nature and the sky will be evicted,
like squatters they have no rights.

When scaffolding arrives, that lyrical
thrush will take his songs elsewhere,
and no passer-by will pause to watch
yellow butterflies explore the ragwort
on mossy ruins, of hearths and lintels ...

Stanley Roger Green

Photograph by Lloyd Smith

Edinburgh International

Before the Apex Hotel
men repair the road. From the East
they work west. Swing doors flash
loosing people in a rush.

The Waverley a kaleidoscope
of carriages slipping out and
in on silver, moving lives to
termini in strange tongues.

The spume of aircraft that cross
the Laws, swoop or lift,
blinking like larks in the sun
while slow tankers froth the Firth.

Edinburgh, imaged in the round
of my startled eye, the song on
my lips, the beat of my step,
my heart, touring the globe.

John Hudson

Edinburgh

So what's to come?
Rebirth by the Forth or super-duper slum?
Conundrum of the coming millennium
In Gilmerton, Liberton, Longstone
                                        or whatever.
Sprawl of splendour no longer
Richly reekin which makes one think and ponder
As to where the lowly workers are.

What? In Pilton, Granton or cultured Craigmiller
Out there somewhere where the regular giro
                                        brings in the siller?

Wonder what Hume, Fergusson or Scott
                                        would have thought
If they'd meditated in some supermarket?
Much food for thought or what as to how so many
Are so easily conditioned, brainwashed and bought
From Arthur's Seat to Princes Street
Manipulated by a shrewd but crude elite
Making money in Merchiston, Marchmont and Craigentinny
Buying and selling as they pile on the agony.
What? Exactly, of course it's not at all funny.

So - on the wane or continuing to grow
With what's to come a tiresome tedium in
                                        a moral vacuum?
Hmm, sorry, being from Glasgow and not Portobello,
How the hell would I know?

Jack Withers

Grassmarket by Michael McVeigh

Impressions of Edinburgh

A silvery skyline,
in the white, misty light
of its giant moon.

Stars suspended up high,
millions of lights above other lights.

Dazzling colours at dawns,
stirring start to the day.
Magical sunsets,
tender invitations to dream.

Streets swept by northernly winds,
a multitude of fragrances
fill the daily air.
From commanding hills
gray gradients run precipitously downwards
and vanish in a glimpse of sea.

This unique city,
which one cannot fail to love.

Laura Fiorentini

Sandy Bell's at Foresthill by Richard Demarco

Biographies

James Adams

Member of Saggar Poetry Group (Dundee) and Scottish Fellowship of Christian Writers. Poems, short stories and articles have been published in many magazines and anthologies.

Meg Bateman

Born in Edinburgh, learnt Gaelic at university in Aberdeen and in South Uist. Shortlisted for the Stakis Prize in 1998. Won a Scottish Arts Council Book Award. Currently teaches at Sabhal Mòr Ostaig in Skye.

Martin Bates

Lives in East Lothian. Writes and translates poetry, as well as writing courses in English as a Foreign Language. Four collections of own poems published. Awarded grant by Government of Mexico to research and translate anthology of contemporary Mexican poetry in Mexico.

Dorothy Baxter

Lives in Edinburgh. Lifelong entertainer. Dance teacher. Children's entertainer. Records tapes for the blind, and performs melody monologues and memories for the elderly. Enjoys bowling.

Robin Bell

Widely published poet and novelist. Grew up in Perthshire, the setting for the best-known of his nine books, *Strathinver: A Portrait Album* 1945-1953. Edited and translated *Bittersweet Within My Heart*, the French poems of Mary Queen of Scots. Latest book - *Scanning The Forth Bridge*.

Sheena Blackhall (Sìne nic Thèarlaich)

Poet, short story writer, singer and illustrator. Published 14 books of poetry and 7 short story collections (mainly in Scots). Currently Creative Writing Fellow in Scots, Elphinstone Institute, Aberdeen University.

Ali Brown

Grew up in Kirriemuir. Studied in Edinburgh in the 1980s, and returned there in 1996, after several years in Aberdeen, Norway and Jerusalem. Works in social research, teaching, shiatsu and counselling.

Christina Brown

Edinburgh born and bred. Currently studying with The Open University and working full-time with the homeless and unemployed in the city.

Elspeth Brown

Full time poet, playwright and novelist. Poetry and short stories published in various anthologies. Member of Solway Festival Poets and Portobello Poets, performing her own poetry with both groups.

Hamish Brown

Widely travelled. Work published in over 100 publications worldwide. Interest in mountaineering and other outdoor activities, as well as being a story teller and poet. Awarded an honorary D.Litt by St Andrews University in 1997.

Margaret Gillies Brown

Born in Edinburgh, now lives in Perthshire. Writing poems for over 25 years; published in many magazines and anthologies. Recently published her autobiography in two volumes - *Far from the Rowan Tree* and *Around the Rowan Tree*.

George Bruce

Published his first collection of poems, *Sea Talk*, in 1944. Of it, Kurt Wittig wrote: "The sea, to Bruce, is a mystic force". His collection, *Pursuit*, won the Saltire Book of the Year Award 1999. His poem, *City Inscape*, carries the idea of "mystic force" to the land.

Tom Bryan

Born in Canada, long-resident in Scotland, including Edinburgh, now living in Selkirk. Widely-published poet and fiction writer. First writer-in-residence for the Scottish Borders.

Ron Butlin

Lives in Edinburgh. His poetry and fiction have gained several Scottish Arts Council Book Awards and many other prizes. His work has been widely broadcast and translated.

Angus Calder

Freelance writer, poet, journalist and historian, living in central Edinburgh. His latest book is *Wars*, an anthology of writing, about European warfare in the 20th century (Penguin).

David Campbell

Born in Edinburgh. Acclaimed international storyteller, writer, broadcaster and poet. Moved from teaching English literature, to producing radio programmes for the BBC, to his third career as a storyteller, carrying the lore of Scottish traditional stories worldwide.

Stuart B Campbell

Originally from Lanarkshire, now lives in Portsoy. Poetry published in a wide variety of literary journals and anthologies; first collection, Robie Gow's Prison (1996). Edited *Things Not Seen - an anthology of Scottish Mountain Poetry* (June 1999).

Jim Carruth

Lives in Renfrewshire. Work published in various publications and anthologies. Winner of Renfrewshire New Poets competition. Commended and published in recent *Arvron International*, *New Writer*, and *The Herald* competitions. Currently working on his first collection.

Beverley Casebow

Born in London, studied at University College London and the University of St Andrews. Works as a museum curator in Edinburgh, and lives in Stockbridge.

Debjani Chatterjee

Award-winning poet and children's writer. Most recent poetry collection: *Albino Gecko* (University of Salzburg Press). Edited *The Redbeck Anthology of British South Asian Poetry* (Redbeck Press).

Tim Cloudsley

Lives in Glasgow, after time spent in other countries. University lecturer in sociology, specialising in the areas of culture, the place of cosmology and myth in society, and society's relationship with the natural environment.

Ken Cockburn

Born in Kirkcaldy, studied at Aberdeen University and University College Cardiff. Currently Fieldworker with Scottish Poetry Library. First collection of poems, *Souvenirs* and *Homelands* (Scottish Cultural Press, 1998), shortlisted for Saltire First Book of the Year Award.

Stewart Conn

Lives in Edinburgh, where for many years he was head of BBC Scotland's radio drama department. Published volume of selected poems, *Stolen Light* (Bloodaxe Books, 1998). Co-edited anthology *The Ice Horses*, (Shore Poets, 1996).

Allan Crosbie

Awarded Scottish Arts Council Writer's Bursary, 1999. Runner-up in 1998 Arvon/Daily Telegraph poetry competition. Poems published in numerous journals, including *The Rialto* and *New Writing Scotland*.

Anna Crowe

Born in Plymouth, now lives in St Andrews. Works in second-hand bookshop and as creative-writing tutor and translator. Prize-winner, National Poetry Competition 1986. Winner, Peterloo Open Poetry Competition 1993 and 1997. Secretary of StAnza 99. Work has been translated into Catalan.

Robert Davidson

Glaswegian living in the Highlands. Contributor of a series of essays on Highland Writers to the Scottish Book Collector magazine. His poem suite Columba was broadcast on Moray Firth radio in April 2000.

Des Dillon

Born in Coatbridge and studied English at Strathclyde University. Writes fiction, poetry, and for stage, film and TV. Awarded Scottish Arts Council Writer's Bursary 1996. Writer in Residence Castlemilk 1997-1999.

Colin Donati

A widely anthologised poet and musician, based in Edinburgh. He received a Scottish Arts Council bursery in 1999.

Hannah Ekberg

American author, from a town named 'Normal'. Has chosen Edinburgh as her adoptive city where she writes, translates for an Internet company, and works as a volunteer at *Chapman* magazine.

Sally Evans

Recently moved to Callander from Edinburgh. Edits *Poetry Scotland* and has had two books and many poems published.

Laura Fiorentini

Born and educated in Italy. British Consulate Milan 1971-1980. Came to Edinburgh 1980. Worked for Italian Institute and, since 1984, for Italian Consulate. Honorary Secretary of Scottish P.E.N., 1986-1998. Has published articles and reviews.

A.M. Forster

Currently works as a poet, reviewer and creative writing teacher. Poems regularly appear in magazines, and in the poetry card *Locked Gardens*. A full-length collection is pending.

Moira Forsyth

Lives in Dingwall. Novelist and poet, first collection of poems and first novel published 1999. Took part with other Highland writers in the organisation of the first Cromarty Book Festival in September 1999.

Victoria Foster

Trained as a nurse and midwife in London. Now living, with her family, amidst the dramatic scenery of the Highlands, the many facets of city life will always fascinate her.

Bashabi Fraser

Born in India, now lives in Scotland. Work published in several anthologies and magazines; first collection: *Life* (Diehard, 1997). Teaches English Literature at the Open University and is a Post-doctoral Fellow at Edinburgh University. Resident Poet in Scotland for Poetry Society.

Valerie Gillies

Widely published poet; publications include *The Chanter's Tune* (Canongate), *The Ringing Rock* (Scottish Cultural Press), and, with artist Will Maclean, *St Kilda Waulking Song* (Morning Star). Enjoys working in the combined arts, with visual artists and musicians.

Sam Gilliland

Born in Ayrshire. Founder/secretary of Ayrshire Writers & Artists Society and co-organiser of Scottish International Poetry Competition. Widely published in the UK and abroad. Exiled in Surrey.

Duncan Glen

Born in Cambuslang, attended Edinburgh College of Art, and lectured in English art schools for many years. Emeritus Professor, Nottingham-Trent University. Returned to Edinburgh, 1987; now lives in Fife. Poetry and prose published since 1960s. Edited *Akros* magazine; currently edits *Zed 2 0*.

Jim Glen

Graduated in English and history, Edinburgh University 1980. Works as a teacher. Many poems and short stories in various magazines and anthologies; also broadcast on BBC Radio. Awarded Scottish Arts Council Writerís Bursaries in 1991 and 1999. Currently working on a novel.

Rody Gorman

Born in Dublin. Published poetry collections in Irish Gaelic and Scots Gaelic, the most recent being Air a Charbad fo Thalamh/ On the Underground (Polygon 2000). Scottish Arts Council Writing Fellow, Sabhal Mòr Ostaig, 1998.

Stanley Roger Green

Born in Edinburgh of 75% Scottish parents (related to Burns). Educated there and Leith Nautical College; thence to circling the world as a cadet on a tramp steamer; finally studying architecture at Edinburgh College of Art.

Jennifer Hadfield

Final year student. Whilst looking forward to studying Creative Writing in Glasgow next year, Edinburgh is her first romance.

Valerie Hawkins

Brought up in poetry-loving family in Finchley. Studied Manchester University. Taught art history, London College of Printing. Lived in Edinburgh for past 20 years. Currently tutors evening classes and works in Edinburgh College of Art Library.

Angela S. Hopkins Hart

A sailor's daughter, has had poetry and fiction published on both sides of the Atlantic, including the poetry collection 'diary of a schizophrenic'. Her dream is to live in Edinburgh.

Tom Hubbard

Published writer and editor; also teaches part-time in Edinburgh College of Art's Humanities Department and Edinburgh University's Centre for Continuing Education. Librarian of Scottish Poetry Library (1984-92) and subsequently taught at universities in France and the USA.

John Hudson

A Londoner, now living in rural Galloway. Poetry published throughout Britain and in Ireland and France. Editor of *Markings* magazine, as well as an arts consultant.

Brian Johnstone

Published in Scotland, Greece and Poland; first collection *The Lizard Silence* (Scottish Cultural Press, 1996). Scottish Arts Council Writer's Bursary 1998. Chairman StAnza Poetry Festival. Forthcoming publication, *Akros*, autumn 2000.

David Keefe

Lives in Bristol. Edits Weatherlight Press and co-leads Wolf at the Door writing workshops. Frequent teacher at Dhanakosa Buddhist Retreat Centre, Perthshire. Currently writing a book on poetry and Buddhism.

S.B. Kelly

Born Falkirk, educated Galashiels and Oxford. Work has appeared in *Poetry Scotland, Northwords, Markings*. Editor of *The Eildon Tree*. Pamphlet, *The Border Cantos*, published by SBC, 1999.

Maurice Lindsay

Glaswegian. Began writing at Glasgow Academy, trained as a musician until the War, after which he became Programme Controller, Border TV. Director The Scottish Civic Trust (now Consultant); Honorary Secretary-General, Europa Nostra (1983-1990). Various publications - poetry and prose.

Christine Lloyd

Retired and a grandmother. Graduated MA(Hons English) from Edinburgh University in 1961. Enjoys attending the Continuing Education Creative Writing Course, and also running her own writers' group.

Christine de Luca

From Shetland, has lived in Edinburgh since student days. Writes in both English and Shetland dialect. Two poetry collections, published by The Shetland Library, each won the Shetland Literary Prize. Has had poems translated into Italian, Swedish and Polish.

Julie McAnulty

Lives in Coatbridge, and is a musician. She is new to writing and has had one other poem published by The Herald as one of the commended entrants in its millennium poetry competition.

Jimmy McCurdie

Born in Portobello. Has been writing short stories since childhood; has recently started writing poetry.

Eilidh MacGregor

Edinburgh born and bred. Graduate of Edinburgh University. Lives and works in the city.

Nancy Macintyre

Retired principal of a special school. Has always written articles and stories, and engages in a huge correspondence. Has only recently started to write poems and belongs to a writers' group in Edinburgh.

Betty McKellar

Born in Edinburgh, now lives in Renfrewshire. Took up poetry-writing as a retirement hobby and has won several Renfrewshire Library and Museum poetry-writing competitions.

Andrew McNeil

Born in Ohio and grew up in Anstruther, Fife. Works as a teacher in Burntisland, and stays in Dunfermline. Currently studying for a Postgraduate Degree at Northern College.

Kevin MacNeil

Widely published writer of poetry, prose and drama. Born and raised in Lewis. Lived in Edinburgh for five memorable years. Inaugural recipient of the Iain Crichton Smith Writing Fellowship (Writer-in-Residence for the Highlands).

Neil mac Neil

Widely published prize-winning poet; writes in Scots and English. Among poets commissioned by MSPs and Scottish Poetry Library Scheme. Former editor of *Strath*. Rich experience of giving readings, workshops and creative writing courses.

Hugh Macpherson

Born in Edinburgh and brought up there before working abroad for many years in the Diplomatic Service. Received the National Library of Scotlandís Robert Louis Stevenson Award in 1998, and was shortlisted for the Poetry Society's Geoffrey Dearmer Award in 1999.

Ken Morrice

Has had eight volumes of poetry published, including *Talking of Michelangelo* (Scottish Cultural Press), and has contributed to many magazines and anthologies.

David Morrison

Born in Glasgow; now lives in Caithness. Poet-painter, short-story writer and Editor of the *Scotia Review*. Lover of Edinburgh.

John Murray

Teaches at Edinburgh College of Art. Work has appeared in various literary publications. First volume: *Aspen* (Akros). *Chiaroscuro* is forthcoming from Diehard. Watermarks is an exhibition of photographs and poems, travelling throughout Scotland.

Tom Murray

Widely published writer from the Scottish Borders. Collection of prose, *Out of my Head*, recently published. Currently on the editorial staff of The Eildon Tree.

Siùsaidh NicNèill

Work published in many anthologies, Scottish and International, as well as magazines. Writes in both Gaelic and English but favours the latter. First collection: *All My Braided Colours* (Scottish Cultural Press, 1996); a second collection is print ready.

Liz Niven

Born in Glasgow, has lived in Galloway since 1983. SAC Bursary 1996. Currently Writer in Residence (Dumfries and Galloway Arts Association) Writes poetry and educational Scots Language materials. Canongate collection due Spring 2001.

Tom Pow

Born in Edinburgh and now lives in Dumfries. Teaches part time at Dumfries Academy. Author of four books of poems, and co-runner of Cacafuego Press.

Alison Prince

Poet, biographer (of Kenneth Grahame and Hans Christian Andersen) and prize-winning writer for children. Lives and works on the Isle of Arran.

Tessa Ransford

Born in India, has lived most of her life in Scotland. Has published 10 books of poems. Founder/director Scottish Poetry Library (1984-1999); founder/organiser School of Poets poetry workshop (1981-99); editor *Lines Review* poetry magazine. Now a roving poetry practitioner and adviser.

James Robertson

Lived much of his adult life in Edinburgh before moving to Fife. Has had two collections of poetry published; first novel, 'The Fanatic', published May 2000. Editor of a new edition of the poems of Robert Fergusson.

Maureen Sangster

Born Aberdeen, currently living in Edinburgh. Poet; also works in the field of mental health. Writer in Residence at Dumfries Royal Infirmary and the Crichton (Jan 1999-Jan 2000) during which time her contribution to this anthology was written.

Caroline Scott

Student of English, Open University, and daughter of Whitbread Award-winning children's author Hugh Scott. Lives and works in Edinburgh; designs fashion accessories.

Paul Henderson Scott

Born in Edinburgh, educated at Royal High School and Edinburgh University. Served in the Army during the War. Diplomatic Service 1947-1980. Has written about 12 books and edited or contributed to about 20 others. President of the Saltire Society.

Sudeep Sen

Published several collections of poetry, most recently *Postmarked India: New and Selected Poems* (HarperCollins, 1997); awarded a Hawthornden Fellowship (UK) and nominated for a Pushcart Prize (US). Writings have appeared in many publications and radio broadcasts. Works as an editor and literary critic; lives in London and New Delhi.

Morelle Smith

Born and raised in Edinburgh; studied at Edinburgh University. Poetry and short stories published in magazines and anthologies. Latest poetry collection: *Deepwater Terminal* (Diehard, 1998). Teacher of English, Creative Writing and Astrology. Currently an aid worker in Albania.

Nancy Somerville

Lives and works in Edinburgh. Work has been published in various magazines and anthologies. Member of 'Shore Poets', an Edinburgh based group which organises regular poetry readings.

Kenneth C Steven

Full-time novelist, poet and children's author with ten books in print. Currently Reader/Writer in Residence for Aberdeen City Council.

Gerry Stewart

Born in the United States, but chose at an early age to become an ex-pat. Lives in Glasgow but commutes daily to Edinburgh. Work has appeared in various magazines and anthologies. Currently trying to find time to finish her first collection.

Martha Modena Vertreace

Poet-in-Residence at Kennedy-King College, Chicago. Fellow at the Hawthornden International Writers' Retreat, and the Writers' Centre Dublin. Diehard published Light Caught Bending and Second Mourning.

Helen Walker

Has written poetry since childhood. Lives in the Highlands but has visited Edinburgh several times - inspired by its beauty and history.

Colin Will

Born in Edinburgh. Librarian with a science background, currently working at Royal Botanic Garden, Edinburgh. First poetry collection: *Thirteen Ways of Looking at the Highlands*, and *More* (Diehard 1996); second collection forthcoming summer 2000.

Jim C Wilson

Now lives in Gullane, East Lothian, after half a century in Edinburgh. Writer in Residence for Stirling District (1989-1991). Won Hugh MacDiarmid Trophy in 1997, and currently teaches Poetry in Practice at Edinburgh University's Centre for Continuing Education.

Robin Wilson

Currently Artistic Director of Theatre Works, Glasgow. Lectures in theatre and acting at both Strathclyde and Glasgow Universities. Has written drama and plays for both BBC radio and TV and several short educational films. Two books of his poetry have been published, and work has appeared in many literary magazines.

Jack Withers

Ex-manual worker, writer and performance-poet. Born in Glasgow. Visits Germany annually as an entertainer, performing his own songs and poetry and works by Robert Burns. Three books published. Works now with Survivors, Poetry Scotland's performance-group.

Edinburgh Tenements by Ernest Lumsden (1883 - 1948)

Acknowledgements

Kirsty Wilson

Graphic Designer

Heritage and Arts Design Section

City of Edinburgh Council

Lloyd Smith

Photographer

Corporate Services

City of Edinburgh Council

and to

Gavin Wallace

and

Ron Butlin

for their help and advice.

Edinburgh: an Intimate City has been printed and
published by The City of Edinburgh Council with subsidy
from the Scottish Arts Council.

The paintings reproduced in this volume are part of The
City of Edinburgh Council Fine Art Collection.

5th November by Carol Robertson